Textual

Criticism

Recovering the Text of the Hebrew Bible

by

P. Kyle McCarter, Jr.

Fortress Press
Philadelphia

Library of Congress Cataloging-in-Publication Data

McCarter, P. Kyle (Peter Kyle), 1945–
   Textual criticism.

   (Guides to Biblical scholarship. Old Testament guides)
      Bibliography: p.
      1. Bible. O.T. —Criticism, Textual. I. Title.
II. Series.
BS1136.M38 1986   221.4'4   86–4388
ISBN 0–8006–0471–7

2525A86   Printed in the United States of America   1–471

Contents

Editor's Foreword

Textual criticism is the oldest and in many respects the most fundamental method of biblical scholarship. All who read or study the Bible necessarily depend upon its fruits. This is the case even for the reader of modern translations, for they rest upon decisions about which text was the basis for the particular rendering into a contemporary language. Resolution of text-critical questions is even more basic for the interpreter of the Bible, for preceding all questions concerning the meaning of the text is the determination of what words it actually contained. That is the issue posed by textual criticism.

One of the most important distinctions to keep in mind as one approaches the issues addressed in this book is the difference between a manuscript and a text. "Text" refers to the contents of the given book or verse, the words written down, while a manuscript—or even a printed Bible—is a particular copy of that text. The same text may be written down or published in many different manuscripts or books, or it may be spoken aloud. In the case of the Hebrew Bible, as with most other books from antiquity, uncertainty and disagreement about the authentic or original or legitimate text arise because it has been transmitted in so many different forms. All these written forms, both Hebrew manuscripts and ancient versions, are witnesses to and evidence for the text.

Since all of those witnesses are more or less "corrupt"—that is, diverge to some extent from a hypothetical earlier text—the goal of textual criticism is to reconstruct the text. One must account for the differences among the witnesses in order to retrace the steps of the ancient scribes, and where possible recover a more original form of the words they wrote down. Like the other methods of biblical criticism, it is a disciplined but creative process. As Kyle McCarter points out, its "rules" are but the application of common sense, and they must not be applied rigidly but with judgment and insight.

This is the second volume in Guides to Biblical Scholarship on Old Testament textual criticism. The other, *Textual Criticism of the Old*

Testament: The Septuagint After Qumran, by Ralph W. Klein, addresses some of the same basic issues of method, but its major concern is to show the implications of the Dead Sea Scrolls for our knowledge of the text. It thus stresses one of the important dimensions of textual criticism, the history of the transmission and development of the text.

The purpose of this volume is to provide a basic introduction to the goals and methods of textual criticism, to give the student of Hebrew sufficient guidance to engage in the process himself or herself. The traditional principles of the discipline are explained in terms of both their usefulness and their limitations. Appendices provide a glossary of technical terms, catalogues of the major textual witnesses to the individual books of the Old Testament, and an evaluation of the characteristics of those witnesses book by book.

Emory University   GENE M. TUCKER
Atlanta, Georgia
October, 1985

8

Abbreviations and Symbols

B.C.E.	before the Common Era (= B.C.)
BHS	*Biblia Hebraica Stuttgartensia*
C.E.	of the Common Era (= A.D.)
LXX	the Septuagint
LXXᴬ	the Codex Alexandrinus
LXXᴮ	the Codex Vaticanus
LXXᴸ	the so-called Lucianic MSS of LXX
MS, MSS	manuscript, manuscripts
MT	the Massoretic Text
MT (K)	the written *(kĕtîb)* form of a word in MT
MT (Q)	the read or vocalized *(qĕrê)* form of a word in MT
OL	the Old Latin version
P.	Papyrus
Targ.	the Targum
[ ]	missing or restored text
⟨ ⟩	text omitted by error
°	reconstructed reading

I

The Art and Science of
Textual Criticism

A. THE NECESSITY OF
TEXTUAL CRITICISM

Erasmus, reacting to criticism of the "new" readings in his edition of the New Testament, likened his detractors to a priest who had a breviary in which *sumpsimus* was misprinted as *mumpsimus*. The old man had become so accustomed to his text that, when the error was pointed out to him, he refused to make the correction and continued to intone *mumpsimus* in the mass for the rest of his life.[1]

Students working in almost any literary field will recognize the devotion of Erasmus's priest. A familiar text seems always to have zealous adherents, who think of the text they know as the authentic text. They can be relied upon to resist any challenge to a traditional reading, even if it is demonstrably corrupt. From their point of view, textual criticism, because it places the traditional text under constant scrutiny, is destructive or (at least) unnecessary. The textual critic, after all, is a scholar who respects neither familiarity nor tradition insofar as texts and readings are concerned. Indeed, he distrusts the familiar, as we shall see. Thus he sometimes seems a disruptive member of the scholarly community, where, insofar as the votaries of *mumpsimus* are concerned, he is unwelcome.

Because of the nature of texts and their transmission, however, the textual critic cannot be excluded from the society of scholars. In the case of a few recent works of literature the autograph (the author's own manuscript) still exists. Under such circumstances the authentication of the text might be a simple matter of collation: If a reading is in doubt, it can be checked against the original.[2] For older literature, however, this is impossible. We seldom have autographs, only copies—usually copies of copies. Because of human

---

1. P. S. Allen, ed., *Opus epistolarum Des. Erasmi Roterodami*, vol. 2 (Oxford: Clarendon Press, 1910), ep. 456.
2. Even in these cases, however, things are seldom so simple. Editorial activities, such as revision and the preparation of new editions, must be considered, so that the determination of the text intended by the author often becomes a highly complicated problem.

fallibility, it is very unlikely that any copy of a long composition will be free of errors, and when the copy is recopied again and again, the unlikelihood quickly becomes absolute. No copy of an ancient composition is pristine. Whenever scholars care about the authenticity of the text they are studying, therefore, textual criticism is necessary.

In one sense, a text is an intangible entity. It is the wording of something written. The text is contained in the written work, but because it can be copied, the text is an independent thing, and when the work perishes, the text survives if it has been copied. At that point the integrity of the text—its fidelity to its original form—depends on the accuracy of the copy. Copying, in other words, is a source of both survival and corruption for a text; the very process that preserves the text also exposes it to danger. When writing is done on perishable materials, as it usually is, the survival of a text over a long period of time is possible only if it is copied many times. It follows that such a text, because it has been exposed so often to the danger of copying, is especially liable to corruption.

Textual criticism is an enterprise that has as its objective the enhancement of the integrity of a text. It is based on the study of the extant copies of the text. The critic compares these copies and attempts to draw conclusions about the divergences between them. The goal is the recovery of an earlier, more authentic—and therefore superior—form of the text.

What I have said so far applies to all texts. The text with which we are now concerned, however, is that of the Hebrew Bible. It survives in an unusually complex form. Copies have been transmitted by rabbinic tradition in an unbroken sequence over the millennia. Other copies—or partial copies—have been discovered at Qumran and other archaeological sites. The Hebrew of the Bible has been translated into numerous other languages, and copies of the translations have been preserved. Each of these copies, whether of the text itself or of a translation of the text, is called a *witness*, inasmuch as it provides testimony to the original form of the text. The biblical textual critic assembles these witnesses and compares them in an attempt to explain their divergences. The goal is the determination of a primitive text to which the various surviving copies bear witness.

Because the integrity of the text is at stake, the textual criticism of the Hebrew Bible can be thought of as an end in itself. It seeks to recover and preserve an authentic text, and thus it requires no other justification. At the same time, however, biblical textual criticism is a means to other ends. It is a preliminary step in the interpretation of the meaning of the biblical text and in the use of the Bible as a tool in the investigation of a variety of topics. Textual criticism, therefore, has a place in almost every activity in which students of the Hebrew Bible engage.

B. IN DEFENSE OF
TEXTUAL CRITICISM

Few modern biblical scholars would dispute the last statement. It is precarious (to say the least) to build a scholarly project on the foundation of an unestablished text: There is always the danger that the foundation might give way at some point where a textual accident has been mistaken for an editorial characteristic or a scribe's idiosyncrasy has been analyzed as the stylistic trait of an author. Proper method requires that, before drawing conclusions, the scholar will call upon all the textual resources and critical acumen available to him in an effort to be as certain as possible that the text from which he is working is authentic and primitive.

In practice, however, many scholars neglect the text-critical task, and a few openly depreciate it. Its validity or necessity is sometimes questioned in academic discussion and publication. In fact, textual criticism is regarded with enough suspicion or hostility among biblical scholars today to require that any treatise devoted to its principles should begin with a statement in its defense. This apologia must address the objections and concerns implied in the following list of mistakes and misconceptions.

1. Some Common Fallacies

a. *Textual criticism is unnecessary when the meaning of MT is clear.* A scholar at work on a biblical passage usually begins by examining the Massoretic Text (MT). Most often he finds that MT reads smoothly, exhibiting no obvious textual difficulty. The notion is widespread that in such a case—that is, when the meaning of MT is clear—there is no reason for recourse to textual criticism. When MT provides an intelligible reading, therefore, no other witness is consulted. Only in the event of apparent trouble in MT will an examination of the versions be undertaken, and even in this case there is a strong preference for some solution to the problem based on an analysis of MT alone.

This notion is erroneous. In the first place, it implies an *a priori* preference for the Massoretic tradition over other textual traditions. One can think of a number of situations in which such a preference might be appropriate, as in a case where the rabbinic-Massoretic Bible was itself the topic of discussion or where it was determined that MT had a claim to authority within a theological tradition under investigation. Ordinarily, however, MT is to be regarded as one witness among others. It will be, to be sure, the only intelligible witness at times, and it will very often be the best among a number of intelligible witnesses. But in no case can the text-critical task be omitted because MT (or some other text) is intelligible. Textual criticism is mandatory whenever more than one reading is found among the various witnesses to the text. And even when there is only one reading, the scholar must reckon with the possibility that it is corrupt.

In the second place, the uncritical adoption of MT when it is intelligible violates one of the fundamental principles of text-critical logic. When we think of a corrupt text, we may automatically think of a garbled or obviously defective reading. On consideration, however, we realize that this reflex is contrary to common sense. A copyist who inadvertently strays from his text is much more likely to write something familiar to himself—something he frequently writes—than something unfamiliar. It is the nature of scribal error that it tends to produce the ordinary, commonplace, or "easy" reading. Corrupt texts, therefore, very often read quite smoothly. Thus the intelligibility of MT (or any other witness) is not an indication that it is textually sound and provides no basis for deciding whether a text-critical investigation ought to be undertaken.

b. *Even when MT seems corrupt, it usually preserves the original reading.* In contemporary biblical studies the presumption in favor of MT is not restricted to situations in which the meaning of MT is easily grasped. In discussion of passages that are textually difficult one often hears the argument that MT's reading, despite its obscurity, *can* be understood without recourse to other witnesses and that those textual critics who have proposed alternative readings have overlooked some way of making MT intelligible. It is pointed out that many features of the ancient Hebrew language (lexical, grammatical, etc.) were unknown to the scribes and translators who passed the text down. The ancient translations and interpretations of the text—including its vocalization by the Massoretes—are not, therefore, trustworthy. Often authentic ancient features of the text were lost when translators distorted them in "correction" toward the narrower confines of a too-limited view of the language.

There is much to commend this point of view. It makes us aware of the long and complex history of the transmission of the text we have, and it encourages us to be wary of the limits of our familiar lexical and grammatical resources. It also has specific value for the textual critic, whom it warns not to dismiss a difficult reading as hopelessly corrupt too quickly. It is fair to say, in fact, that the critic must now include within his inventory of requisite skills a thorough grounding in the historical development of the Hebrew language and in comparative Northwest Semitic philology.

It does not follow from all of this, however, that there should be a gain in the presumption of superiority accorded any one text. Certain Massoretic readings once thought corrupt might now be recognized as distinctive, authentic, and primitive. But the same might be true of the *Vorlage* of one of the versions at any given point—and this with equal possibility. Moreover, as James Barr and others have insisted, the application of the data of Northwest Semitic philology to the biblical text must be undertaken with great care and reserve.[3] The broader one casts his philological net, the greater the number of linguistic phenomena he can count among his catch—and the more difficult the problem of responsible selection.

The analogy of the Arabic lexicon may be instructive here. When struggling with an obscure word in a Northwest Semitic inscription, I find that after the Hebrew, Aramaic, Phoenician, Ugaritic, and even Akkadian dictionaries are exhausted, I can still turn to an Arabic dictionary and—if the particular edition I have chosen is a large one—hope to find "evidence" for a meaning that suits my fancy as well as the context. But the Arabic lexicon is so vast and varied in comparison to the lexica of the research languages of antiquity that etymologies drawn from it are notoriously facile. And so is the application of features of the grammar of Ugaritic and other Northwest Semitic languages to the interpretation of the biblical text. It must be done, but it must be done carefully.

c. *Textual criticism is of no importance.* Even among those scholars who have no bias toward MT there are many who regard textual criticism as unnecessary. They find MT a perfectly satisfactory text, and, though they might accept the legitimacy of a text-critical argument in principle, they do not believe that the emendation of MT ever leads to any result that is important for biblical interpretation.

Because this attitude is found among scholars in most literary fields—wherever tradition has lent authority to some widely followed text—it may be useful for gaining perspective to glance at an analogous situation outside the realm of biblical studies. Shakespeare scholars rely primarily on the Folio (F), generally the best preserved witness to the text of the plays. F, in other words, enjoys roughly the same authority for the Shakespearean corpus that MT has for the Hebrew Bible. Modern textual analysis, however, has identified numerous places where other witnesses display readings superior to those of F. Several years ago, Fredson Bowers of the University of Virginia, having been invited to address the English Institute at Columbia, called his audience's attention to this situation. Among other things, he presented the evidence that Shakespeare wrote "O that this too too *sullied* flesh . . .," as preserved in the second quarto of *Hamlet* (Q2, which actually reads "sallied"), rather than "O that this too too *solid* flesh . . .," the reading of F ("sollid").[4] He went on to lament the tendency in modern editions of

3. Barr, *Comparative Philology and the Text of the Old Testament* (Oxford: Clarendon Press, 1968).
4. The argument was later published as "Hamlet's 'Sullied' or 'Solid' Flesh: A Bibliographical Case-History," *Shakespeare Survey* 9 (1956):44–48. For Bowers's own account of the reaction to his proposal, see chap. 1 of his *Textual and Literary Criticism* (Cambridge: Cambridge University Press, 1966). His *Bibliography and Textual Criticism* (Oxford: Clarendon Press, 1964) is the standard work on the textual criticism of *printed* books.

Hamlet to rely on the text of F to the neglect of superior readings in other witnesses, citing a number of other passages where Q2 has readings that are superior to those of F.

The first respondent to Bowers's paper reacted with indignation and impatience. He found "solid" to his liking and, in any case, could see nothing to be gained from trying to discover which Shakespeare wrote, which was of no importance; the "essential values" of *Hamlet* were unaffected.

We may wonder with Bowers, however, how many unsound readings can be tolerated in the text of a play by Shakespeare—or a portion of the Bible—before the "essential values" *are* affected and before scholarly hypotheses built upon the text are vitiated. In the case of "sullied" or "solid," the answer to this question is probably not even one, because the issue of interpretation at stake was whether or not Hamlet means to say that his flesh is tainted by inheritance from his mother.

d. *The results of textual criticism are minimal.* This is a less extreme expression of the last opinion. It reflects the view that the gains of textual criticism are slight. The scholars who hold this view admit that text-critical arguments may occasionally have exegetical importance. They point out, however, that the scintillating emendation that illuminates a previously obscure passage is extremely rare. Most textual work is tiresome and unrewarding. From this point of view, then, textual criticism is not "cost efficient"—that is, very great effort is required for very small gains.

Such a sentiment is most understandable in scholars whose work concentrates on those parts of the Bible where the textual resources are least generous—where the textual data are most uniform or simply opaque. In such books, textual criticism can be tedious, frustrating, and generally futile. But a sense of the triviality of text-critical research is not confined to these contexts; it is expressed with reference to texts where several variants confront the critic in every verse and compete for his favor.

It is true that the recovery of a spectacular variant—one that alters some area of our knowledge in a single stroke—is rare, and the announcement of such a discovery should always be received with reserve. But text-critical progress is made in small steps, not in great leaps. The spectacular archaeological discovery is equally rare, but it is not through the publication of sensational finds that the archaeologist contributes to biblical studies. For the archaeologist—and the textual critic—it is not the individual discovery, be it spectacular or banal, that he expects to yield important conclusions; rather, it is the sum of a large number of discoveries, most of them banal, that he turns to when it is time to draw conclusions. Data gathered from countless small finds, patiently catalogued, classified, and analyzed, are the basis of his arguments.

While preparing the textual notes for my commentaries on 1 and

2 Samuel[5] I kept the issue of triviality in mind. I did not suppose that anyone would think it trivial that a scroll of Samuel from Qumran (4QSam^a) has a paragraph about Saul's Ammonite war missing from all other extant witnesses, that the Septuagint has a longer reading in 1 Samuel 14 providing considerable detail on the otherwise obscure institution of the Urim and Thummim, or that some witnesses deny that "the sons of David were priests" (cf. 2 Sam. 8:18). I did wonder, however, whether I might be accused of triviality for reporting my choice between *wayyō'mer dāwid*, "and *David* said," and *wayyō'mer hammelek*, "and *the king* said," a report I made many times in *II Samuel*. Is this a trivial decision? In a given passage it may seem so, but the sum of such passages might say something about courtly style or literary history or something else impossible to anticipate. I assume that no one acquainted with modern source criticism thinks the choice between *wayyō'mer yahweh*, "and *Yahweh* said," and *wayyō'mer hā'ĕlōhîm*, "and *God* said," in a Pentateuchal passage is a trivial matter. And finally, how trivial is the integrity of the text itself?

e. *Textual criticism is arbitrary.* The concern here is that the data necessary to a textual decision are so numerous, intricate, and elusive that rigorous textual work seems almost impossible. The result of this concern is a suspicion that text-critical decision making is arbitrary and unscientific, that a textual decision, when it comes, comes from the heart rather than the head.

This suspicion is not a new one, and long ago textual critics responded to it by attempting to place their work on a fully scientific basis. They formulated fixed rules by which textual choices can be made. Many of these rules are still familiar; they radiate most authority when proclaimed in Latin. *Lectio difficilior praeferenda est*, "The more difficult reading is to be preferred." This rule is based on the observation that scribal errors tend in the direction of the familiar: A scribe is much more likely to "see" and substitute a familiar synonym for an obscure word than the reverse. *Lectio brevior praeferenda est*, "The shorter reading is to be preferred." This rule follows from the recognition that a text subject to intense scribal activity tends to expand by conflation, glossing, dittography, and so on.

The trouble with such rules is that they cannot stand the test of rigid application. Difficult readings, for example, can be preferred only up to a point. Occasionally a textual accident produces garbage. The "more difficult reading" is not to be preferred when it is garbage. The most common scribal error (I think) is haplography, that is, reading two identical sequences of letters as one and omitting whatever intervenes. What then of the *lectio brevior* when it is the result of such an accident?

5. Anchor Bible, vols. 8 and 9 (Garden City, N.Y.: Doubleday & Co., 1981, 1984).

Is it true, then, that textual criticism is arbitrary? Is the preferred reading really the *lectio pulchrior* (the reading better suiting the aesthetic tastes of the critic) or the *lectio convenientior* (the reading more compatible with the critic's higher-critical arguments)?

No. The textual criticism of the Hebrew Bible is a discipline with integrity and rigor. In Chapter III, when we take a closer look at the classic rules (including the rules of the more difficult reading and the shorter reading), we shall see that they are invaluable tools. Properly understood, they are not laws but guidelines, reminding the critic of what he has learned about the characteristics of textual corruption and curbing his less rational impulses. It is true that these guidelines cannot be applied woodenly, but this is because in the last analysis textual criticism is as much an art as it is a science.[6] The scholar must wield all its tools with the deftness and delicacy of an artist. And, like any artist or scientist, he must ply his trade with intelligence and common sense. Good textual criticism is, above all, a matter of good judgment, and the good textual critic, while he will most often possess both creativity and learning, is most characteristically identifiable by the soundness of his judgment.

It follows that textual criticism is not arbitrary. Every decision the critic makes must be able to withstand what A. E. Housman once described as "the application of thought." But this brings us to our next topic.

C. HOUSMAN'S DOG

The student preparing to do textual work must acquire considerable philological training, he must learn the general guidelines for textual criticism, and he must acquaint himself with the characteristic forms of textual corruption. None of this, however, will enable him to do effective textual reconstruction if he does not also cultivate the proper attitude toward his task. This is a lesson that must be learned by every new generation of textual critics—especially in a time, like our own, when the emphasis in the study of the text seems to be on the manipulation of highly technical resources and the invocation of arcane principles.

It was at a similar juncture in the textual study of the literature of ancient Greece and Rome that A. E. Housman offered the following advice to the Classical Association:

A man who possesses common sense and the use of reason must not expect to learn from treatises or lectures on textual criticism anything that he could not, with leisure and industry, find out for himself. What the lectures and treatises can do for him is to save him time and trouble by presenting to him immediately considerations which

---

6. In a superb paper on recent Septuagint research read to the Society of Biblical Literature on December 18, 1982, Albert Pietersma expressed the opinion that textual criticism is "certainly as much an art ... as ... a science."

would in any case occur to him sooner or later. And whatever he reads about textual criticism in books, or hears at lectures, he should test by reason and common sense, and reject everything which conflicts with either as mere hocus-pocus.

Housman was reminding his colleagues that the key to good textual work is finally common sense. The title of his paper was "The Application of Thought to Textual Criticism."[7] He was in favor of it (i.e., the application of thought) but found himself in a minority position. Instead of thought (common sense, good judgment, etc.), he found scientific principles applied —statistical hypotheses, probability theories, and highly specialized skills (he especially noted palaeography, which was very much the vogue among classical scholars at the time). He had no quarrel with these methods in themselves, but he regarded them as worthless when employed by a textual critic who is prejudiced or stupid.

The danger in the use of scientific principles is that of applying generalizations to individual problems. The scholar who knows that something is generally or usually true is naturally inclined to suppose that it is true in the particular case he is considering. As we shall see, such a supposition should never be made by the textual critic. Housman used a memorable metaphor to stress this point:

A textual critic engaged upon his business is not at all like Newton investigating the motion of the planets; he is much more like a dog hunting fleas. If a dog hunted for fleas on mathematical principles, basing his research on statistics of area and population, he would never catch a flea except by accident. They require to be treated as individuals; and every problem which presents itself to the textual critic must be regarded as possibly unique.

The student who hopes to become a competent textual critic cannot hope for better advice than that given by Housman. The starting point in good textual work is the cultivation of the proper critical attitude, and this attitude is grounded in two simple ideas, which the student should keep constantly in mind. First, the only absolute laws in textual criticism are the laws of reason and logic. Second, these laws must be applied to every textual problem individually and afresh.

It is true that the aspiring textual critic, even if he cultivates the proper critical attitude, cannot be certain he will succeed. Some of us lack the natural gifts necessary to the task. As Housman expressed it: "If a dog is to hunt for fleas successfully he must be quick and he must be sensitive. It is no good for a rhinoceros to hunt for fleas: he does not know where they are, and could not catch them if he did." Fortunately, however, it is unusual for a student to be so thick-skinned that he cannot hope to become a competent textual critic. If he will emulate Housman's dog, skeptical of scientific principles and generalizations, pursuing his task reasonably, and treating

7. Published in the *Proceedings of the Classical Association* 18 (1922):67–84.

every case as an individual, he will have an excellent chance of achieving his goal.

D. SOME GENERAL GUIDELINES

It follows from what we have already said about the limited value of general principles that the student of textual criticism is likely to learn more from examples than advice. The sampling of textual data offered in Chapter II, therefore, should be given primary attention. Nevertheless, it may be helpful at this point to offer a set of general guidelines, if only to serve as points of reference to which the student can return to remind him of the things the examples teach him.

These guidelines contain two kinds of advice. First are those things that ought to be done by the student who is preparing himself to do textual criticism. Second are those things he should keep in mind when actually engaged in the restoration of a text.

1. Guidelines for Preparation

a. *Be sure you are competently trained in the skills.* The emphasis in the preceding remarks on the importance of common sense should in no way be interpreted as disparagement of the technical skills of the text-critical craft. The languages and other tools are, to state the obvious, absolutely essential. If I have neglected this fact so far, it is only to stress the point that expert control of these skills cannot make a good textual critic of a scholar who does not apply them sensibly. The skills themselves, however, are (in a word) prerequisite.

A minimal list of the skills necessary for text-critical work in the Hebrew Bible would include the following:

Languages (primary): Hebrew, Greek, Aramaic, Syriac, Latin

Languages (secondary): Coptic, Ethiopic, Armenian, Arabic

Hebrew philology: historical grammar, orthography, paleography

The student who finds this list discouraging may take some comfort from the assurance that his training in the secondary languages will not be called upon very often in the course of routine textual work. To be sure, the Armenian text, for example, will occasionally prove essential to the pursuit of some text-critical project. In such a case, however, it is important to remember that the study of the biblical text is a venture upon which a fairly large community of scholars is at work. Someone will be found to read the Armenian.

On the other hand, some of the entries in the list that seem harmless may prove formidable when encountered on the text-critical field of battle. The thoroughly drilled student of Greek, for example, though well prepared for the linguistic onslaughts of Plato, on the one hand, and Luke-Acts, on the other, is in for a shock the first time he engages a sturdy passage of Septuagint. At the same time, his training in historical Hebrew grammar is incomplete unless it includes a knowledge of the development of the language over more than a millennium of its use and an acquaintance with the essential features of closely related languages, such as Ugaritic. And while the text-critical knight-errant may be able to trudge along if his Armenian is rusty, he will be brought to a halt if he cannot joust successfully with a hostile passage of Septuagint, and he may lose his way entirely if he is unfamiliar with the terrain of the standard Ugaritic lexicons.

b. *Familiarize yourself with the characteristic forms of textual corruption.* The kinds of mistakes that occur when a manuscript is being copied are more or less the same whether the language of the text is Biblical Hebrew, English, or something else. There are, therefore, certain clearly defined categories of error, and the textual critic needs to be familiar with them all. There are several ways to accomplish this. One is to type your own papers. This is an effective method, but very slow unless you are an unusually careless typist. A better way is to study Chapter II.

c. *Learn the one great rule.* Although we shall examine several rules for choosing between readings, they all boil down to one. It is usually expressed in one of two ways, both formulated by the great New Testament critics of the eighteenth century and still followed by textual critics in all fields. These are (a) *Difficilior lectio potior*, "The more difficult reading is preferable," and (b) *Utrum in alterum abiturum erat?* "Which would have been more likely to give rise to the other?"

The rule is probably best known to biblical scholars in a variant of the first form, *Lectio difficilior praeferenda est*, "The more difficult reading is to be preferred," as cited above. This is a misunderstood rule, because "the more difficult reading" is an imperfect translation of *lectio difficilior* as those who first promoted the principle intended it. It is not simply the harder reading that is to be preferred, but the more distinctive. We want the reading that is suitable, sensible, and elegant. We do not want the commonplace reading (if we have an alternative), but neither do we want garbage.

The other form of the rule *(Utrum in alterum . . .)* is akin to this. A common, familiar reading is unlikely to have given rise to an unusual, elegant, distinctive equivalent; the reverse is more likely to have been the case.

As the student will quickly recognize, this rule, in whatever form it is expressed, is only common sense formalized, and when its application conflicts with common sense—as it occasionally will—it must be set aside without embarrassment or regret. There is, after all, some truth to the reductionist and somewhat cynical opinion that all such rules boil down to one truism, namely, *Melior lectio potior*, "The better reading is preferable."

d. *Sit at the feet of a master.* All of these guidelines, though they may help you discipline your work, will not sharpen your critical faculties. To do this you must sit at the feet of a master. This is possible even if you have already finished your formal training and your present colleagues are text-critical rhinosceri of the sort lamented by Housman. Somewhere in the literature of the research into most parts of the Bible there is a study in which a truly gifted critic has worked through the text and published some of his results. To read the work of such a critic is to learn more than can be set down in any kind of manual for doing textual criticism.

As I worked through 1 and 2 Samuel, I was constantly aware of the advantage of being able to consult Wellhausen. This advantage was not that his notes on the text of Samuel provided numerous solutions to difficult problems (though that, too, was true) but that I could always keep him before me as a model of what it was I was supposed to be doing. I often disagreed with his specific conclusions and, more often, found no help from him on particular problems. But he was almost always rational and sensible as a textual critic, and he was immensely talented. Contrast him with the other great commentators on the text of Samuel: Thenius, Wellhausen's own inspiration, who was brilliant but undisciplined; Klostermann, who was prodigiously erudite but whose common sense often abandoned him; Budde, who too often gave in to his prejudices; Henry Preserved Smith, who was earnest but lacking in any real text-critical dexterity; and Driver, who was usually good, but at his best in the *Notes on Samuel* when paraphrasing Wellhausen's German in English.

When you work on a text, find your Wellhausen and read him for inspiration.

2. Rules of Application

a. *Keep a clear image of the scribe in mind.* Our readings, all of them, come from scribes. Every extant witness to the biblical text passed under the hands of many scribes in antiquity. Some of these fellows were sharp and industrious. More were dull and indolent. They were, after all, human beings. They were fallible, apt to make mistakes out of carelessness, laziness, stupidity, senility, drunkenness, fatigue, or general incompetency. They were, in short, much like you and me. And they made the same mistakes we make when we type our papers. It is important to be familiar with the kinds of mistakes they characteristically made, and, as I have already suggested, you can discover what these are by studying Chapter II—and by proof-reading your papers.

The other thing to remember about a scribe is that he punched a time clock and drew his wages on Friday for copying manuscripts. Nobody paid him a nickel for anything else. He was not an author. He was not an editor. He was not a censor. He was a copyist. Hence the next guideline.

b. *Look first for the unconscious error.* The better solution to a textual problem—when one solution assumes a textual accident and another an intentional alteration—is the first. Even the great scholars of the text forget this advice too often. Textual criticism is a rational activity, and there is a temptation to rationalize the changes that occurred in the text. The fact is, however, that deliberate alterations of the text were rare in antiquity, and textual accidents were common. The critic who thinks in terms of inadvertent errors, therefore, will do the more effective job of restoring the text.

Most of the time, then, it is good to keep the picture of the scribe as a dedicated copyist in mind, assuming that when he altered his text it was by accident rather than design. Occasionally, however, this picture must be banished or it will mislead the critic. For it is not true, after all, that scribes never intentionally changed their texts, that secondary readings never arose out of tendentious tampering with a manuscript. The text of the Hebrew Bible has been deliberately altered in a few places, as examples cited in Chapter II.D will show.

c. *Know the personalities of your witnesses.* Manuscripts have personalities. The witnesses in a textual court of law are individuals, and the critic (*kritēs*, "judge") who is called upon to decide a case based on their evidence must become well acquainted with each of them.

If the critic is fortunate, all his witnesses will be healthy, reliable, and forthcoming. In that case the evidence he requires will be fairly easy to obtain. At least as often, however, the witnesses to a text will be ailing, untrustworthy, or uncooperative. Some, for example, will be old and spare. In consequence of their age and experience, they may have valuable testimony to give; but they will often be debilitated and unable to give it freely, and the critic will have to be patient and alert when interrogating them. In contrast, other witnesses will be grinning, overweight youngsters, more than willing to testify on every subject. They will tend to be full of pranks and hyperactive, and the critic may find it difficult to keep them quiet while he deliberates. Between these two extremes are other types of witnesses who, despite a reliable appearance, will prove no less troubling to the critic. Some will seem to have no mind of their own, incessantly parroting the testimony of one or another of their companions. Others will promise to provide valuable evidence but wander away at the precise moment they are needed. Unfortunately the critic cannot afford to ignore any of these individuals, however exasperated he may become, because it is possible that any one of them might harbor the secret that will solve his case.

When preparing a text-critical case, therefore, you should cultivate acquaintances of this kind. Become familiar with your particular circle of witnesses. Most especially, learn how they behave in immediately adjacent texts. This will enable you to weigh the evidence given by one against the other. For example, if two witnesses almost always agree in the adjacent material, then their agreement in your passage may be insignificant. But if they seldom agree elsewhere, then their agreement in your passage is probably important. But you will find it hard to evaluate their agreement or disagreement if you are not familiar with the pattern of their relationship elsewhere.

This advice, like other generalizations, can lead you astray. This is one of the reasons for the next guideline.

d. *Treat each case as if it were unique.* This is one of the lessons we learn from Housman's dog, and its importance has been recognized for a long time. The eighteenth-century German historian August Ludwig von Schlözer, one of the pioneers in the modern study of texts, thought of it as the one universally valid principle of textual criticism.

The behavior of a given set of witnesses in a given situation is unpredictable. One or more may be momentarily "out of character." We are, after all, dealing with human frailties. As we have seen, textual criticism is necessary primarily because of ancient mistakes. One cannot expect a mistake to follow fixed rules. If the mistake was in the habit of following rules, it would never have qualified as a mistake in the first place. It would have been drummed out of the Mistake Academy and enrolled as just another trivial instance of correctness and good behavior. I may think of the Lucianic witnesses to Samuel as full texts and MT as tending toward haplography. But I must always be alert to the possibility in a given case that LXX[L] is parableptic and MT is intact. This is, of course, possible in a given case, and since every case is a given case, it is possible in every case.

This is another one of those facts apt to be forgotten even by the textual specialists—I might say especially by the specialists, because it is they who are most likely to be well acquainted with general textual characteristics. A scholar who has written the definitive study of something—let us say (to be on the safe side) Theodore of Mopsuestia's recension of the Megilloth or the character of the Samaritan witness to Joshua—is quite likely to find evidence confirming his conclusions in a given passage in Ruth or Joshua. This sort of prejudice is hard to avoid. If you have not yet written a definitive monograph on a textual phenomenon, you are safe from this prejudice for the time being. If you have produced such a study, remember that your thesis is no less correct in general if it is wrong in an instance or two. The logical principle of the counterexample does not work in textual criticism. If your thesis is that Jerusalem became literate first during the reign of Josiah, the Siloam tunnel inscription is a problem for you. But if your thesis is that St. Ambrosia's text of Qoheleth tends to be defective, one or two batches of overstuffed Ambrosian Ecclesiastes is no threat to you. You are safe this time. But for you, and also for those of us whose *curricula vitae* tend to be thin in the definitive monograph column, there are other prejudices to be avoided. Hence the next rule.

e. *Beware of prejudices.* Because textual criticism, as Housman and others insist, requires reason and good judgment, it is especially vulnerable to prejudices. It has no resistance to them. Prejudice is fatal to textual criticism.

Erasmus's priest preferred the familiar text of his own breviary regardless of its merit. Similarly, there are modern biblical scholars who prefer the reading of MT regardless of its scientific merit, and there are others who seem ready to embrace any reading that disagrees with MT regardless of its merit. There are those who will defend any reading that supports their theories or the theories of their teachers, and there are those who will reject any reading that supports the theories of their rivals. All of these scholars, in one way or another, are votaries of *mumpsimus.* They are all prejudiced, and they cannot hope to produce enduring critical work.

f. *Apply thought to textual criticism.* This is Housman's rule, but not his alone. Richard Bentley, one of the great New Testament critics of the eighteenth century, expressed it in the form it deserves, a Latin apothegm: *Ratio et res ipsa centum codicibus potiores sunt,* "Reason and the facts are preferable to a hundred manuscripts." When applied assiduously, this rule renders the others unnecessary.

II

The Causes of
Textual Corruption

How did the biblical text become corrupt? In antiquity the books of the Bible were recorded on scrolls. Both the leather from which the scrolls were made and the ink with which the texts were written were perishable. Even if a scroll escaped accidental damage, it would eventually wear out and become illegible or too fragile to use. Therefore a fresh copy had to be made from time to time.

Ironically enough, it was this periodic copying, which was intended to preserve the integrity of a text, that rendered the text subject to corruption. This was true because of the universal fallibility of the manual reproduction of a text. Manual copying, whether accomplished with the aid of a stylus or a keyboard, is a cooperative enterprise involving the hand, the eye, and the brain—each of which is inclined to play tricks on the others. Although these tricks are not predictable, they do fall into general patterns determined by the mechanical requirements of the copying process. For this reason, it is possible to categorize textual mistakes according to various risks to which an ancient copyist was subject.

The types of textual corruption according to which this chapter is organized, therefore, are in no way peculiar to the biblical text. They can be found in the history of the transmission of any literature, and textual critics in all fields of study are familiar with them. Each of them is illustrated here, however, by examples drawn from the text of the Hebrew Bible.

A. CHANGES THAT EXPAND THE TEXT

The types of textual corruption may be divided into three categories, namely, those that expand the text, those that shorten the text, and those that do not affect the length of the text. Changes that expand the text are treated first here, because it is corruption of this kind that the textual critic ought to suspect first. This is because of the principle of *Brevior lectio potior*, "The shorter reading is preferable," or *Lectio brevior praeferenda est*, "The shorter reading is to be preferred." This principle arises from the determination of the ancient scribes to transmit their texts fully intact. In their care to omit nothing, they were likely to preserve all kinds of glosses, marginal notes, and insertions. Thus texts, especially those that were frequently copied, tended to expand, and the critic in search of the primitive form of a text is wise to regard longer readings with suspicion.[1]

1. Simple Expansion

By "simple expansions" we refer to intrusions into the text that did not result from mechanical accidents, such as dittography, or from the deliberate inclusion of additional materials, as in the case of glossing or the conflation of variant readings. Simple expansions are those that arose spontaneously during the copying of a text; the text was enlarged without the intention or even the awareness of the scribe.

What specific forms did such expansion take? This question is best answered by an examination of some portion of text that displays expansionistic tendencies. A good choice would be the MT of Joshua, a text that appears very full when compared to that of the LXX. The MT of Joshua contains numerous intrusive words and phrases, and it is often conflate, combining more than one reading in a single passage. These are marks of intense scribal activity over a long history of transmission. The beginning of Joshua, therefore, provides several examples of simple scribal expansions, some of which are detailed below.

a. Intrusive Words Providing Clarity or Emphasis

A common way in which a scribe might unintentionally enlarge his text was by the addition of words that (1) provided grammatical precision or clarity—most often particles (*'t*, etc.), relative pronouns or conjunctions (especially *'šr*), and the conjunction *l'mr*—or (2) added emphasis (*kl, m'd,* etc.). Note the following examples.

Josh. 1:7   MT   חזק ואמץ מאד

              LXX =   חזק ואמץ

The adverb *m'd* adds emphasis ("*very* sturdy and strong"), but its absence in LXX shows it to be secondary.

Josh. 2:3   MT   לחפר את כל הארץ

          LXX, Syr. =   הארץ   לחפר את

Again the intrusive word, *kl*, makes the statement more emphatic ("to spy out *all* the land").

Josh. 9:24   MT   אשר צוה יהוה אלהיך את משה עבדו   את

         MT^MSS   את כל אשר צוה יהוה אלהיך את משה עבדו

This is another case where *kl* has intruded into the text of some witnesses:

---

1. The principle of *lectio brevior* is further discussed in Chapter III. As in the case of other text-critical guidelines, this principle ought to be discarded in cases where it misleads. A short text may be primitive, but it may also be defective, as the examples in part B below illustrate.

"everything that Yahweh your god commanded Moses his servant." In this case it is MT that preserves the shorter reading: *"that which* Yahweh. . . ."

b. Intrusive Clichés

The critic will often find a portion of the biblical text expanded with stereotyped or frequently repeated words or phrases. These expressions occurred automatically to the scribe because of his familiarity with the language of the Bible, and they often found their way into his text. Common titles or epithets, for example, attached themselves easily to names.

Josh. 1:1, 15   MT   משה עבד יהוה   Moses, the servant of Yahweh

            LXX =   משה   Moses

Moses' title "servant of Yahweh" was used for the first time in the immediately preceding material (Deut. 34:5). It occurs in both MT and LXX in Josh. 1:13 and several other times throughout the book (8:31, 33; 11:12; 12:6 [first occurrence]; 13:8; 14:7; 18:7; 22:2, 5). It is not surprising, therefore, to find it added to Moses' name in the MT of Josh. 1:1, 15 and other verses (12:6 [second occurrence]; 22:4), where its absence from LXX shows it to be secondary.

Josh. 1:15   MT   ושבתם לארץ ירשתכם וירשתם אותה אשר נתן לכם משה

and you will return to the land of your possession—
and you will take possession of it—which Moses gave you

LXX = אשר נתן לכם משה   ושבתם איש אל ירשתו

and you will return, each to his own possession, which Moses gave you.

The expression *wyrštm 'wth,* "and you will take possession of it," has no counterpart in the text of LXX. It belongs to the stock of stereotyped language used in this material in reference to the occupation of the land by the Israelites. Thus it arose, either spontaneously or as a misreading of the preceding *yrštkm,*[2] "your possession," here in Joshua's instructions to the soldiers of Reuben, Gad, and Manasseh. But it is unsuited to this context, where the land referred to has already been captured, and its absence from the text of LXX shows it to be secondary.

c. Additions Under the Influence of Other Parts of the Passage

Sometimes a scribe added words remembered from another part of the passage he was copying. Thus when similar phrases occurred in different parts of the same passage, they tended to become more similar or identical, as the following example illustrates.

2. If the latter explanation of its origin is correct, it should be classified as a corrupt variant or duplicate rather than a simple expansion.

28

Josh. 2:16   MT   עד שוב הרדפים

LXX   ἕως ἂν ἀποστρέψωσιν οἱ καταδιώκοντες ὀπίσω ὑμῶν

= עד שוב הרדפים אחריכם

The expression "until those who pursue have returned" was expanded in the *Vorlage* of LXX to read "until those who are pursuing *after you* have returned." A scribe added the extra word in reminiscence of *hrdpym 'hryhm*, "those who are pursuing after them," in v. 7 (cf. v. 5).

Another example from the same chapter shows, again, that similar parts of a passage tended to influence each other. Note that in this case, however, the scribe was influenced by a reading that appeared later on in his text. Thus the critic should be alert not only for expansions made *in reminiscence* of other parts of a passage, as in the preceding example, but also for expansions made *in anticipation* of other parts of a passage.

Josh. 2:9   MT   וכי נמגו כל ישבי הארץ מפניכם

These words, which are not represented in the text of LXX, are part of Rahab's speech to Joshua's spies in MT: "I know that Yahweh has given you the land and that the dread of you has fallen upon us *and that all the inhabitants of the land are trembling before you.*" The source of the expansion in this verse can be found at the end of the chapter, where the spies make their report to Joshua. Joshua 2:24 reads: "They also said to Joshua, 'Yahweh has given all the land into our hand, and indeed all the inhabitants of the land are trembling before us'" *(wgm nmgw kl yšby h'rṣ mpnynw)*. The similarity between the two speeches caused a scribe to expand v. 9 in anticipation of v. 24.

2. Dittography

Dittography, "double writing," occurs when a scribe unintentionally repeats part of his text. It may involve a single letter or several words.

a. Simple Dittography

Here is an example of simple dittography found in the great Isaiah scroll from Qumran.

Isa. 31:6   MT   שובו לאשר   העמיקו

Return to him against whom (the Israelites) have profoundly (transgressed).

1QIsaᵃ   שובו לאשר לאשר העמיקו

The scribe of the scroll copied the second word, *l'šr*, "to him (against whom)," twice. The original shorter text is preserved in MT.

Simple dittography of this kind is sometimes found in MT, as in the following examples, taken from the rabbis' list of biblical readings that are to be "written but not read" *(kĕtîb wĕlō' qĕrê)* cited in the Talmudic tractate Nedarim 37b–38a.

Jer. 51:3   MT   אל ידרך ידרך הדרך קשתו

Let not [?] the archer draw *draw* his bow![3]

Ezek. 48:16   MT   ופאת נגב חמש חמש מאות וארבעת אלפים

and the south side five *five* hundred and four thousand

Sometimes several words were involved in dittography, as in the following examples.

Lev. 20:10   MT   ואיש אשר ינאף את אשת איש אשר ינאף את אשת רעהו מות

ימות הנאף והנאפת

And as for the man who commits adultery with the wife of *a man who commits adultery with the wife of* his neighbor, he shall be put to death, both the adulterer and the adulteress.

A scribe inadvertently repeated the sequence '*yš* '*šr yn'p* '*t* '*št*, and the extraneous words were preserved by subsequent copyists. The shorter original reading is reflected in the text of some manuscripts of LXX.

Ezek. 16:6   MT   ואעבר עליך ואראך מתבוססת בדמיך ואמר לך בדמיך חיי ואמר

לך בדמיך חיי

When I passed by you and saw you weltering in your blood, I said to you in your blood, "Live!" *And I said to you in your blood, "Live!"*

Here the repeated words were *w'mr lk bdmyk ḥyy*. Again the shorter original text is preserved in the versions, in this case LXX and Syriac.

Sometimes it is possible for the critic to identify the cause of simple dittography. The following passage provides a good illustration.

2 Kings 7:13   MT   ויען אחד מעבדיו ויאמר ויקחו נא חמשה מן הסוסים הנשארים

אשר נשארו בה הנם ככל ההמון ישראל אשר נשארו בה הנם

ככל המון ישראל אשר תמו ונשלחה ונראה

One of his servants answered and said, "Let five of the remaining horses be taken, for those who remain here will be like the whole multitude of Israel *for those who remain here will be like the whole multitude of Israel* who have perished. So let's send them and see."

In this case the repeated sequence, '*šr nš'rw bh hnm kkl h[h]mwn yśr'l*, is missing in the texts of the major versions as well as many manuscripts of MT. The dittography occurred because of the repetition of the word '*šr* at the beginning of the phrases '*šr nš'rw* and '*šr tmw*. It is a case, in other words, of dittography caused by *homoioarkton*. A scribe's eye skipped back from the second '*šr* to the first, causing him to repeat several words.

3. It is possible that this is not a case of dittography but rather a combination of two readings, namely, '*l ydrk*, "let him not draw," and *ydrk*, "let him draw."

b. Dittography Compounded by Other Errors

The kind of simple dittography illustrated by the preceding examples was easy for the scribes to identify and correct. Though it might occur often in the copying of a single manuscript, such as 1QIsaᵃ, it is less likely to have been preserved and passed down in an ongoing manuscript tradition. For this reason, simple dittography is less common in the major witnesses to the Hebrew Bible than dittography compounded by other errors. These other errors—most often the corruption or displacement of the repeated sequence—created circumstances in which dittography was not easily recognized as such and was more likely, therefore, to be preserved.

Sometimes the double writing became corrupt, as in the following case.

1 Sam. 20:3   MT   עוד דוד

               LXX = דוד

In this passage *dwd*, "David," seems to have been written twice in a text ancestral to that of MT. The first *dwd* was then misread as *'wd*, "again," and the dittography was preserved in this corrupt form. As often happens, the resulting confusion gave rise to other problems that trouble the text of MT in this passage.

In other cases, dittography escaped correction and survived because the dittograph (the repeated sequence of letters) was displaced, as in the following example.

Isa. 64:2   MT   ירדת מפניך הרים נזלו

                      You came down. Before you the mountains quaked.

These four words, which occur in Isa. 63:19, were copied twice by a scribe, a case of simple dittography. A subsequent scribe found the repeated sequence floating free in the text, so to speak. He did not recognize the words as extraneous and, in his confusion, attached them to the end of the next line of his text.

Often the critic will be able to discover why a part of a text was repeated in another place. Usually the trigger was a word or a sequence of letters that occurred in both places, as in the following examples.

2 Kings 11:17   MT   ויכרת יהוידע את הברית בין יהוה ובין המלך ובין העם להיות

                                             לעם ליהוה ובין המלך ובין העם

                   Jehoiada cut a covenant between Yahweh and the king and the people, so that they should become a people of Yahweh—*and between the king and the people.*

The sequence *wbyn hmlk wbyn h'm*, which appears at the end of the verse in MT, was marked by Origen with an asterisk, indicating that it was missing from his Greek text (cf. LXXᴸ and the synoptic passage in 2 Chron. 23:16). It is a repetition of the same sequence earlier in the verse. This dittography was triggered by the word *yhwh*, which precedes the repeated words in both places.

Ezek. 36:14–15 MT לכן אדם לא תאכלי עוד וגויך לא תכשלי עוד נאם אדני יהוה¹⁴

ולא אשמיע אליך עוד כלמת הגוים וחרפת עמים לא תשאי¹⁵

עוד וגויך לא תכשלי עוד נאם אדני יהוה

¹⁴Therefore you shall no longer devour men, and your nation you shall no longer totter. Oracle of my lord Yahweh. ¹⁵And I will no longer make you hear the contempt of the nations, and the reproach of the peoples you shall no longer bear. *And your nation you shall no longer totter.* Oracle of my lord Yahweh.

The sequence *wgwyk l' tkšly 'wd* in v. 15 is repeated from v. 14. In this case, the word *'wd*, which precedes this sequence in both places, probably triggered the dittography. Note that the shorter original text is preserved by both LXX and Syriac.

When a sequence of words repeated in a nearby passage displays some variation from the first occurrence, the critic may suspect that the repetition arose from a scribe's desire to preserve two readings known to him. The following passage is a case in point.

Isa. 17:12–13 MT ושאון לאמים כשאון מים כבירים ישאון ¹³לאמים כשאון¹²

מים רבים ישאון

¹²and the roar of peoples—like the roar of mighty waters they roar ¹³*of peoples—like the roar of many waters they roar.*

The repeated sequence may have arisen in order to preserve the variants *kbyrym* and *rbym*. Note that if this is true, the expansion in these verses does not represent an authentic case of dittography.

3. Glossing

A gloss is any kind of explanatory information added to a text by a scribe. Generally speaking, the purpose of such an addition was to remove ambiguity or avoid misunderstanding in a passage the scribe perceived as insufficiently clear. Some specific reasons for the introduction of glosses are illustrated by the examples that follow.

a. To Explain Obscure Terms

Obscure or archaic words were sometimes glossed with familiar words intended to explain them. Consider the following examples.

Gen. 7:6 MT והמבול היה מים על הארץ

And the flood was *water* upon the earth.

A scribe glossed the rare noun *mbwl*, "flood," by adding *mym*, "water." We suspect *mym* of being secondary not only because it is lacking in LXX but also because of the grammatical awkwardness of the resulting reading. Compare Gen. 6:17, where the same gloss has been introduced in all witnesses.

Zech. 6:3　　　MT　　ובמרכבה הרביעית סוסים ברדים אמצים

> And with the fourth chariot were dappled *glimmering* horses.

The rare word *brdym*, "speckled, dappled" (cf. Gen. 31:10–12), was glossed as *'mṣym*, "glimmering" (not "strong"). For us this is an even rarer word (cf. Arabic *wamaḍa*, "flash, gleam"), but it must have been more common in the language of the scribe.

Josh. 20:3　　　MT　　רוצח מכה נפש בשגגה בבלי דעת

The passage concerns the establishment of the cities of refuge as an asylum for "one who commits manslaughter, taking a life unintentionally." In MT the expression *bšggh*, "inadvertently, unintentionally," is explained by the phrase *bbly d't*, "without knowledge." The absence of *bbly d't* in LXX and the Vulgate, however, shows the words to be a scribal gloss.

Ps. 28:3　　　MT　　אל תמשכני עם רשעים ועם פעלי און

In this verse LXX displays an example of a *displaced* gloss, adding *mē synapolesēs* = *'l t'bdny*—thus, "Do not drag me off [?] with the wicked, and with those who do evil *do not destroy me!*" The extra words probably arose in the margin as an explanation of the difficult verb *'l tmškny*, but the gloss was eventually inserted into the text in a position that gives the semblance of poetic parallelism.

b. To Explain Unusual or Obscure Statements

Another type of explanatory gloss was sometimes introduced to clarify an odd or confusing passage.

Josh. 2:15　　　MT　　ותורדם בחבל בעד החלון כי ביתה בקיר החומה ובחומה היא יושבת

> She let them down *with a rope* through the window *(for her house was in the city wall and it was in the wall that she lived)*.

This verse belongs to the story of Rahab and the spies of Joshua. The italicized material is lacking in the text of LXX. It was introduced at some point in the development of MT by a scribe who thought the original statement, "She let them down through the window," required explanation. If the city gate was shut (cf. v. 7), how did the spies escape the city after climbing out of the window of Rahab's house? The scribe added an epexegetical gloss, explaining that Rahab's house was built into the city wall.

2 Sam. 11:4　　MT　　והיא מתקדשת מטמאתה
　　　　　　　4QSam^a　　והיא מתקדשת

This verse says of Bathsheba at the time of her adultery with David that "she was purifying herself." To this a scribe added "from her uncleanness" as an explanatory gloss. The absence of *mṭm'th* in the Qumran scroll shows it to be secondary in MT.

c. To Identify Obscure or Ambiguous Place-names

Scribes often glossed the names of places that were not well known, that were better known by another name, or that shared a name with another place. The following example illustrates the last of these three situations.

Jer. 43:13   MT   את מצבות בית שמש אשר בארץ מצרים

           LXX   τοὺς στύλους Ἡλίου πόλεως τοὺς ἐν Ὤν

             =   את מצבות בית שמש אשר באן

The passage refers to shattering *'t mṣbwt byt šmš*, "the pillars of Beth-shemesh," that is, the Egyptian city of On, or Heliopolis. To avoid confusion with the Beth-shemesh of Judah, the place-name was glossed *'šr b'rṣ mṣrym*, "which is in the land of Egypt," in the tradition ancestral to MT and *'šr b'n*, "which is in On," in the tradition lying behind LXX.

The critic will find that glosses on place-names often appear in all witnesses to a given reading. In such a case, it may be impossible to determine whether the gloss is scribal and secondary or a contribution of the original author or editor of the passage. Occasionally, however, other criteria will cast doubt on the originality of a gloss, as in the following case.

Gen. 35:19; 48:7 MT   בדרך אפרת[ה] הוא בית לחם

These passages refer to the burial of Rachel "on the way to Ephrathah, that is, Bethlehem." All witnesses share MT's gloss identifying Ephrathah with Bethlehem (cf. Ruth 4:11; Micah 5:1; 1 Chron. 4:4). In addition to Ephrathah in Judah, however, there seems to have been a district called Ephrathah in the vicinity of Kiriath-jearim in Benjamin (cf. Ps. 132:6; 1 Chron. 2:50), and 1 Sam. 10:2 suggests that it was with this northern Ephrathah that Rachel's tomb was originally associated. The glosses in Genesis, therefore, seem to be erroneous and thus probably secondary.

d. To Make the Implicit Explicit

Scribes frequently expanded texts to express what was implied (see A.4, below). In the following examples this expansion takes the form of explicitating glosses attached to nonspecific terms or phrases.

Josh. 6:26   MT   את העיר הזאת את ירחו

According to this verse, Joshua pronounced a curse upon the man who would rebuild "this city." The context shows that the city referred to is Jericho, but at some stage in the development of MT a scribe felt it necessary to make this explicit and added *'t yrḥw*. The gloss is absent from the text of LXX.

Ezek. 44:7   MT   בהביאכם בני נכר ... להיות במקדשי לחללו את ביתי

> When you admit strangers ... to my sanctuary to profane it, *that is, my temple.*

The words *'t byty* were introduced by a scribe who wanted to be sure the reader understood that the profanation of the temple was at stake.

e. To Qualify Generalizations

Scribes perceived some general statements to be open to misunderstanding and qualified them with glosses. A scribe's purpose in such a case was to protect his text from misinterpretation and ensure conformity with other passages. Consider the following examples.

Exod. 22:19   MT   זבח לאלהים   יחרם בלתי ליהוה לבדו

Samaritan   זבח לאלהים אחרים יחרם

The original reading was *zbh l'lhym yhrm*, "He who sacrifices to gods will be placed under the ban." The implicit meaning of "gods" was "other gods," that is, other than Yahweh. At some point in the development of MT a scribe felt it necessary to make this meaning explicit and added the gloss *blty lyhwh lbdw*, "except to Yahweh alone." Note that although the text of the Samaritan Pentateuch lacks MT's gloss, it has been expanded by the insertion of *'hrym* with the same result: "He who sacrifices to *other* gods will be placed under the ban."[4]

Josh. 11:19   MT   לא היתה עיר אשר השלימה אל בני ישראל בלתי החוי
ישבי גבעון

> There was no city that made peace with the Israelites *except the Hivites dwelling in Gibeon.*

The phrase *blty hhwy yšby gb'wn* is lacking in LXX. It is a gloss introduced for the sake of precision, bringing the statement into conformity with the account of the Gibeonite alliance in Joshua 9.

f. To Extend the Meaning of a Passage

Contrast the preceding examples with the following, in which a scribe has glossed a passage in order to extend the meaning of the text.

Exod. 21:28, 36

Samaritan   28וכי יכה שור או כל בהמה את איש או את אשה ... 35וכי יגף
שור איש או כל בהמתו את שור רעהו או כל בהמתו

> 28If a bull *or any animal* kills a man or a woman . . .35 and if a man's bull *or any animal of his* harms his neighbor's bull *or any animal of his.*

The italicized portions of the translation are lacking in MT. They are glosses, introduced to make it clear that the law concerning goring bulls (MT has

---

4. Alternatively, one could argue that the Samaritan preserves the primitive text, *'hrym* having fallen out after *l'lhym* by *homoioteleuton*, necessitating the introduction of the gloss in MT.

ygh, "gores," for Samaritan *ykh*, "smites, kills") extended to other animals. For the same reason *bhmh*, "animal," has frequently been substituted for *šwr*, "bull," in the Samaritan text elsewhere in this passage.

4. Explicitation

As we noted in the discussion of explicitating glosses (A.3.d, above), scribal activity tended to make the implicit explicit. Explicitation is a type of expansion that gives expression to something that was only implied in the original text. The following example is typical.

Gen. 29:25   MT   ויאמר אל לבן

LXX   εἶπεν δὲ Ιακωβ τῷ Λαβαν

Here the primitive situation is represented by MT: "And he said to Laban. . . ." The subject, Jacob, is not expressed. In LXX or its *Vorlage*, however, it has been inserted. Explicitation of this kind is extremely common in various witnesses to the Hebrew Bible. It could be classified as a type of simple expansion (A.1, above), inasmuch as it involves additions to the text that seem to have arisen spontaneously and unintentionally. Contrast, however, the following example.

Isa. 42:1   MT   הן   עבדי אתמך בו   בחירי רצתה נפשי

LXX =   הן יעקב עבדי אתמך בו ישראל בחירי רצתה נפשי

Behold *Jacob,* my servant, whom I uphold!
Israel, my chosen one, with whom my soul is pleased!

Here again the name "Jacob"—and also "Israel"—has been added to the text to express something that was not expressed in the original. In this case, however, the expansions are less likely to have been spontaneous than deliberate. That is, the inserted names represent a scribe's attempt to render his text more intelligible according to his own interpretation of its meaning, which he derived from nearby passages (41:8; 44:1; 45:4; etc.). This kind of explicitation could be classified as a gloss (A.3, above; especially A.3.d).

5. Conflation

Conflation is a combination of readings, and a composite text is said to be conflate. Conflation results when variant readings exist and are copied together into the text or when material properly belonging elsewhere is attracted into the text.

a. Conflation of Variant Readings

Sometimes the textual traditions passed down more than one reading of a given word, phrase, or clause. Ordinarily, such variant readings, as they are called, were similar or identical in meaning. Some differed only in grammatical form or syntax. If only one word was involved, the variants might be synonyms; in the case of longer variants, they might be synonymous phrases or clauses. Often one variant will have been preserved in one textual tradition and a second variant in another. Sometimes, however, two or (rarely) more variant readings were preserved in a single, conflate text.

2 Sam. 22:43   MT   אדקם ארקעם

          LXX^B =   אדקם

          4QSam^a ארקעם

The variants here are '*dqm*, "I crushed them," and '*rq'm*, "I mashed them." The first is preserved alone in LXX^B, the second in a scroll from Qumran. Both are combined in the conflate text of MT.[5] As the following example from the same poem shows, conflation of this kind often led to secondary corruption when the scribes attempted to smooth the text and accommodate both readings.

2 Sam. 22:38–39 MT   עד כלותם ואכלם

          4QSam^a עד כלותם   (so Ps. 18:33)

          LXX = עד (אשר) אכלם

The variants '*d klwtm*, "until finishing them," and '*d ('šr) 'klm*, "until I finished them," were combined in MT, where the text was adjusted grammatically—thus, '*d klwtm w'klm*, "until finishing them. And I finished them. . . ."

Isa. 62:7   MT   עד יכונן

          1QIsa^a עד יכין ועד יכונן

This is a simpler instance of the same phenomenon. The grammatical variants '*d ykyn* and '*d ykwnn*, both "until he establishes, sets up," were preserved in the text of the scroll, and the abruptness of the combination was smoothed by the insertion of *w-*, as if "until he establishes *and* until he sets up."

2 Sam. 21:22   MT   להרפה בגת

          LXX   τῶν γιγάντων ἐν Γεθ τῷ Ραφα οἶκος

          = להרפה בגת להרפה בית

The awkward Greek translation, "of the giants in Gath, to Rapha a house," reflects a conflation of variants of which the second arose as a corruption of the first, *bgt* having been read *byt* by confusion of *g* and *y* (C.1.e, below).

Jer. 44:24   MT   כל יהודה אשר בארץ מצרים

                   all of Judah who are in the land of Egypt

Jer. 44:26   MT   כל יהודה הישבים בארץ מצרים

                   all of Judah who *dwell* in the land of Egypt

Though they differ in only one word, both of these long variants were preserved in the tradition ancestral to MT. The absence of the phrase in the

---

5. LXX^L and Ps. 18:43 have '*rqym*, "I poured them out," a corruption of '*dqym* by confusion of *d* and *r* (cf. C.1.f, below).

LXX of v. 24 shows that v. 26 was its original location. The variant now in v. 24 was probably preserved marginally until it was brought into the text in the wrong place.

b. Attraction and Assimilation

Another cause of conflation was the influence of one part of the text on another. This occurred when something in the text of one passage brought another passage to mind, so that elements of the second passage were attracted into the first.

Gen. 17:14	MT	אשר לא ימול את בשר ערלתו
	Samaritan	אשר לא ימול את בשר ערלתו ביום השמיני

This passage excludes from Abraham's family any male "who is not circumcised in the flesh of his foreskin." The reading of the Samaritan Pentateuch, which is shared by LXX, further stipulates that this is to take place "on the eighth day," a specification attracted into the text from Lev. 12:3.

Josh. 20:3   MT   והיו לכם למקלט מגאל הדם
And they will be for you a refuge from the avenger of blood.

LXX = והיו לכם הערים למקלט ולא ימות הרצח מגאל הדם
And *the cities* will be for you a refuge *and the manslayer will not be put to death* from the avenger of blood.

Num. 35:12   MT   והיו לכם הערים למקלט מגאל ולא ימות הרצח
And the cities will be for you a refuge from the avenger, and the manslayer will not be put to death.

In LXX, the "cities of refuge" passage in Joshua has been assimilated to that in Numbers.

Ps. 72:17   MT   ויתברכו בו
LXX = ויתברכו בו כל המשפחת האדמה
The expression *wytbrkw bw*, "They will find their blessing in him," attracted *kl hmšpḥt h'dmh*, "all the families of the land," from Gen. 12:3 and 28:14 into the textual tradition lying behind LXX.

B. CHANGES THAT SHORTEN THE TEXT

Like other text-critical rules, the principle of *lectio brevior* is not an absolute law. The shorter text is not to be preferred when it is defective. There were several kinds of textual accidents that resulted in losses of material. When the critic finds evidence of such a loss, he is justified in supposing a longer reading to be superior.

1. Haplography

Haplography, or "single writing," takes place when a repeated sequence of letters is copied only once with a resulting loss of text. This phenomenon occurred frequently during the transmission of the biblical text, as the following examples illustrate.

Judg. 20:13   MT(K)   ולא אבו בנימן

  And Benjamin were not willing.

    MT(Q)   ולא אבו בני בנימן

  And *the sons of* Benjamin were not willing.

The plural verb shows that the original text read *bny bnymn*, as represented by the *qěrê* with the support of many manuscripts and the versions. The text of the Leningrad Codex, the basis of *BHS*, is defective. Haplography occurred when the repeated sequence of letters *bny* was copied only once. It is easy to see that the expression *bny bnymn* was especially liable to haplography; the same accident has afflicted the texts of numerous other passages, including 2 Sam. 2:15, 31; 4:2; 1 Chron. 7:6; 11:31; etc.

Gen. 19:33   MT   בלילה הוא

    Samaritan   בלילה ההוא

In the original text, here preserved by the Samaritan Pentateuch, *h* was written three times in a row. The solecism now in MT arose when one *h* was omitted as a result of haplography.

Deut. 15:14   MT   ומיקבך אשר

    Samaritan   ומיקבך כאשר

The original sense of this verse, reflected in LXX as well as in the Samaritan Pentateuch, was, "You must provide for him from your flock, from your threshing floor, *and from your wine press; just as* Yahweh your god has blessed you, you will give to him." In MT the sequence *-k k-* led to the haplographic loss of one *k*.

Sometimes haplography involved sequences of letters that were similar in form though not identical. The following case was a result of the graphic similarity of *b* and *k* (cf. C.1.a, below).

2 Sam. 18:20 MT(Q)   כי על בן המלך מת

      MT(K)   כי על כן בן המלך מת

The intended meaning, "For it was because the king's son was dead," was obscured in MT when haplography occurred. Owing to the similarity of *k* and *b*, *kn* was lost in MT before the following *bn*.

2. Parablepsis

Parablepsis, "oversight" or "faulty seeing," occurred when a scribe over-looked part of his text. Most often, this happened when his eye skipped from the sequence of letters he was copying to an identical or similar sequence farther on in the text. Any letters or words standing between the two sequences were lost. In such cases, then, parablepsis involved the "single writing" of two letters or groups of letters and can be considered a type of haplography. Here are several examples, the first of which is taken from the rabbis' list of biblical readings that are to be "read but not written" *(qĕrê wĕlō' kĕtîb)*, cited in the Talmudic tractate Nedarim 37b.

Jer. 31:38   MT   הנה ימים (באים) נאם יהוה

> Behold, the days are coming (oracle of Yahweh).

A scribe's eye skipped from *-ym* in *ymym* to *-ym* in *b'ym* with the consequent loss of *b'ym*.

1 Sam. 12:8   MT   ויזעקו אבותיכם אל יהוה   כאשר בא יעקב מצרים

              LXX = כאשר בא יעקב מצרימה ויענם המצרים ויזעקו אבותיכם אל יהוה

> When Jacob went to Egypt, [the Egyptians oppressed them,] and your fathers cried out to Yahweh.

The original form of the text of this passage is reflected by LXX. Parablepsis occurred in a manuscript ancestral to MT when a scribe's eye skipped from *mṣrymh* to *mṣrym* and the words *-h wy'nm mṣrym h-* were lost.

Parablepsis is an especially significant phenomenon for the study of the biblical text, because, in contrast to most other textual accidents, it frequently resulted in an extensive loss of material, as the following example shows.

Judg. 16:13–14 MT   ¹³... ויאמר אליה אם תארגי את שבע מחפלות ראשי עם

                       המסכת ¹⁴ותתקע ביתד

          LXX =   ¹³... ויאמר אליה אם תארגי את שבע מחלפות ראשי עם

          המסכת ותקעת ביתד אל הקיר וחליתי והייתי כאחד האדם

          ¹⁴ותישנהו ותארג את שבע מחלפות ראשו עם המסכת

          ותתקע ביתד

> ¹³And he said to her, "If you weave *the seven braids of my hair with a web* [and fasten it to the wall with a pin, I'll grow weak and become like any man." ¹⁴So she put him to sleep and wove *the seven braids of his hair with a web*] and fastened it with a pin.

The shorter text of MT is the result of parablepsis in a text identical to that reflected by LXX. A scribe's eye skipped from *'t šb' mḥlpwt r'šy hmskt* to *'t šb' mḥlpwt r'šw hmskt*, identical sequences except for the variation of the graphically similar letters *y* and *w* (cf. C.1.i, below) in *r'šy*, "my head," and *r'šw*, "his head." Everything enclosed in brackets in our translation was omitted.

a. Homoioarkton

When the sequence that triggered the accident stood at the beginning of the lost material, the omission is said to have been caused by *homoioarkton* or *homoeoarchton*, "like beginning." Consider the following example.

Gen. 31:18   MT   אשר רכש מקנה קנינו אשר רכש בפדן ארם

         LXX, Syr. = בפדן ארם   אשר רכש

The verse says that Jacob drove off all his livestock, "which he had acquired, [the cattle that were his own property, which he had acquired] in Paddan Aram." The material represented by the words enclosed in brackets was lost in a text ancestral to that of LXX because of *homoioarkton*. Parablepsis occurred when a scribe's eye skipped from the first *'šr rkš* to the second.

b. Homoioteleuton

When the trigger sequence stands at the end of the lost material, the omission is said to have been caused by *homoioteleuton* or *homoeoteleuton*, "like ending." *Homoioteleuton*, which occurs more frequently than *homoioarkton*, is illustrated by the following examples.

Lev. 15:3   MT   טמאתו הוא   רד בשרו את זובו או החתים בשרו מזובו

Samaritan   רד בשרו את זובו או החתים בשרו מזובו טמא הוא כל ימי זב

בשרו או החתים בשרו מזובו טמאתו הוא

> Whether his flesh runs with his discharge *or his flesh is obstructed because of his discharge*, [he will be unclean as long as his flesh discharges *or his flesh is obstructed because of his discharge*]; it is his uncleanness.

The longer text of the Samaritan Pentateuch (reflected also by LXX) preserves the original reading. The repeated sequence *'w hḥtym bśrw mzwbw*, "or his flesh is obstructed because of the discharge," at the end of the first two clauses led to the loss of the words enclosed in brackets in our translation.

Josh. 21:35–37   MT^MSS   ^35 ... ^36 ואת מגרשה ערים ארבע

^37 ... ואת מגרשה ערים ארבע

Verses 36–37 are entirely missing in the Leningrad Codex and other major manuscripts of MT. They can be restored from other manuscripts of MT and the versions. The cause of their omission in MT was *homoioteleuton:* Verses 35 and 37 ended with the same sequence, *w't mgršh 'rym 'rb'*, "and its common land—four cities."

1 Sam. 14:41   MT   הבה תמים   יהוה אלהי ישראל

LXX =   יהוה אלהי ישראל למה לא ענית את עבדך היום אם יש בי או

ביונתן בני העון הזה יהוה אלהי ישראל הבה אורים ואם ישנו

בעמך ישראל הבה תמים

> O Yahweh god of *Israel!* [Why have you not answered your servant today? If this guilt is in me or my son Jonathan, O Yahweh god of Israel, give Urim! But if it is in your people *Israel*,] give Thummim!

In the original form of this speech by Saul—which is preserved with slight variations in LXX, the Peshiṭta, and the Old Latin—the word *yśr'l* was repeated three times. A long passage was lost from MT when a scribe's eye skipped from the first *yśr'l* to the third.

41

Isa. 4:5–6   MT   ⁵ ... ענן יומם ועשן ונגה אש להבה לילה כי על כל כבוד חפה
⁶וסכה תהיה לצל יומם מחרב

1QIsaᵃ   ⁵ ... ענן יומם ⁶מחרב

⁵ ... a cloud *by day* [and smoke and the shining of a flaming fire by night, for over all glory there will be a shelter. ⁶And there will be a booth for shade *by day*] from the heat.

The trigger in this example was *ywmm,* "by day." Several words were lost from the text of the Qumran scroll when a scribe's eye skipped from the first *ywmm* to the second. The longer, original reading is preserved in MT.

A final pair of examples is taken from chap. 3 of Ruth, where the word *'ly,* "to me," has been lost twice, once because of *homoioteleuton* (v. 5) and once because of *homoioarkton* (v. 17).

Ruth 3:5   MT   כל אשר תאמרי ⟨אלי⟩ אעשה
Everything you say to me I will do.

Ruth 3:17   MT   כי אמר ⟨אלי⟩ אל תבואי ריקם
For he said to me, "Don't go away empty-handed."

Both of these examples are cited in the list of words to be "read but not written" in Nedarim 37b.

3. *Other Omissions*

The critic posits a loss of material most confidently when he is able to point to some mechanism, such as haplography or parablepsis, to account for the omission. We must suppose, however, that the scribes occasionally overlooked parts of their text without an apparent cause. The critic, therefore, will sometimes find himself suspecting that the longer of two readings is original even though he cannot offer a mechanical explanation for the shorter text. Consider the following familiar example.

Gen. 4:8   MT   ויהי   ויאמר קין אל הבל אחיו
בהיותם בשדה

Samaritan   ויאמר קין אל הבל אחיו נלכה השדה ויהי
בהיותם בשדה

And Cain said to his brother, Abel, "Let's go outside." And when they were outside. . . .

The longer reading of the Samaritan Pentateuch has the support of the versions. There seems to be no mechanical explanation for the loss of *nlkh hśdh,* "Let's go outside," however, and under such circumstances the critic ordinarily prefers the shorter reading even when numerous manuscripts are lined up on the other side. In this case, however, the longer reading is generally believed to be original. The absence in MT of any speech after "And Cain said to his brother, Abel" is very awkward, and the reading of the Samaritan is precisely what we expect.

Ps. 145:13+ versions = נאמן יהוה בכל דבריו וחסיד בכל מעשיו

> Faithful is Yahweh in all his words,
> and loyal in all his deeds.

Psalm 145 is an acrostic poem, each of its verses beginning with a different letter of the Hebrew alphabet. In MT, however, there is no *nun* verse between v. 13, which begins with *mem*, and v. 14, which begins with *samek*. The missing verse is supplied by the versions and a scroll from Qumran (11QPsᵃ). Should we restore v. 13+? Against such a reconstruction are the absence of a mechanical explanation for the loss of the verse, the similarity of the reading preserved in the versions to the words of v. 17, and the occasional absence of verses beginning with various letters in other acrostic poetry. Nevertheless, most modern critics, feeling the need for a *nun* verse in the psalm, have given preference to the longer text of the versions.

C. CHANGES THAT DO NOT AFFECT
THE LENGTH OF THE TEXT

Not all changes affect the length of the text. There are various mistakes and substitutions that leave a reading in corrupt condition without substantially lengthening or shortening it. Such changes occurred frequently during the transmission of the biblical text in antiquity.

1. Graphic Confusion

Scribes sometimes miscopied words because they mistook certain letters for others that were similar in form. When the critic encounters variant readings that diverge in only one or two letters, therefore, he should consider the possibility of graphic confusion. It is obvious that those pairs of letters that most closely resembled each other were most liable to confusion, and many of the most frequently confused pairs (*dalet* and *reš*, *he* and *ḥet*, etc.) can be predicted from an acquaintance with the forms of the letters that appear in modern Hebrew Bibles. A reliable assessment of the likelihood that any given pair of letters might have been confused, however, is only possible on the basis of a familiarity with the scripts in which the biblical manuscripts were transmitted in their full development from the fourth century B.C.E. to the first century C.E. The critic who suspects graphic confusion, therefore, should have recourse to comparative charts of these scripts.[6]

---

6. The standard work is F. M. Cross, "The Development of the Jewish Scripts," in *The Bible and the Ancient Near East: Essays in Honor of William Foxwell Albright*, edited by G. E. Wright (Garden City, N.Y.: Doubleday & Co., 1965), 170–264. For the paleo-Hebrew script, see R. S. Hanson, "Paleo-Hebrew Scripts in the Hasmonean Age," *Bulletin of the American Schools of Oriental Research* 175 (1964):26–42, with supplementation and correction in his study of "Paleography" in D. N. Freedman and K. A. Mathews, *The Paleo-Hebrew Leviticus Scroll (11QpaleoLev)* (ASOR; Winona Lake, Ind.: Eisenbrauns, 1985), 15–23.

The following list includes examples of the most frequently confused pairs of letters.

a. כ / ב

Isa. 63:6   MT   ואשכרם בחמתי

MT^{MSS}   ואשברם בחמתי

And I *made them drunk/shattered them* in my anger.

The preceding stich, *w'bws 'mym b'py*, "And I trampled peoples in my wrath," commends the second reading.

Hos. 9:4   MT   ולא יערבו לו זבחיהם

And their sacrifices will not be pleasing to him.

MT^{MSS}   ולא יערכו לו זבחיהם

And they will not set sacrifices in order for him.

It is difficult to choose between these readings. To the first may be compared Jer. 6:20, but the second has been preferred by many modern critics in the light of the parallel stich, *wl' yskw lyhwh yyn*, "They will not pour out wine to Yahweh."

Job 21:13   MT(Q)   יבלו בטוב ימיהם

MT(K)   יכלו בטוב ימיהם

They *use up/complete* their days in prosperity.

Again, it is difficult to choose between these readings. The versions support the *qĕrê*.

Eccl. 5:16   MT   גם כל ימיו בחשך יאכל

Yes, all his days he eats in darkness.

LXX =   גם כל ימיו בחשך ואבל

Yes, all his days are in darkness and gloom.

Here the confusion involved two pairs of letters, *waw* and *yod* (see C.1.i, below) and *bet* and *kap*. The reading of LXX is superior. The confusion in MT was probably abetted by the references to eating and drinking in v. 18.

b. מ / ב

Isa. 11:15   MT   והחרים יהוה את לשון ים מצרים

LXX =   והחריב יהוה את לשון ים מצרים

And Yahweh *will destroy/dry up* the tongue of the sea of Egypt.

Isa. 38:9   MT   מכתב לחזקיהו מלך יהודה

emendation   מכתם לחזקיהו מלך יהודה

A *writing/miktam* of Hezekiah king of Judah.

Though the witnesses to this passage unanimously reflect *mktb*, "a writing," it has long been suspected that the original reading was *mktm*, "a miktam" (cf. Ps. 16:1; 60:1; etc.).

Hab. 1:17   MT   העל כן יריק חרמו
                        Will he therefore empty his net?

        1QpHab   על כן יריק חרבו
                        Therefore he will draw his sword.

In this case the reading found in the pesher from Qumran is superior. In MT, *bet* and *mem* were confused under the influence of the reference to *ḥrmw*, "his net," in vv. 15 and 16.

c. ב / נ

Amos 7:14   MT   בוקר
      emendation   נוקד [cf. Amos 1:1]

Though the second reading has no clear support from any witness to the text, it enjoys wide support in modern scholarship. Note that if this emendation is correct, we have an instance of the confusion of *nun* for *bet* and *dalet* for *reš* (see C.1.f, below) in a single word.

d. ג / ו

Ruth 4:5   MT   ומאת רות
       versions = גם את רות

According to some versions, Boaz says to Naomi's kinsman, "On the day you buy the field from Naomi, *also Ruth* the Moabite widow you buy." This seems better than MT's reading, "and [= also?] from Ruth," which probably arose by confusion of *gimel* and *waw*.

2 Sam. 23:36   MT   יגאל   Igal
1 Chron. 11:38   MT   יואל   Joel

The reading of Chronicles, also reflected by LXX^L in 2 Sam. 23:36, is plainly inferior. The substitution of the common name "Joel" for the rare "Igal" was abetted by the graphic similarity of *gimel* and *waw*. Note that the same confusion exists in the Greek text of 1 Chron. 3:22, where LXX has *iōēl* = *yw'l* corresponding to MT *yg'l*.

e. ג / י

2 Sam. 21:22   MT   להרפה בגת
      LXX = להרפה בגת להרפה בית

LXX reflects a conflate Hebrew text, combining variants that arose from confusion of *gimel* and *yod*. See the discussion under A.5.a, above.

f. ד / ר

Because *dalet* and *reš* closely resembled each other in the scripts of most periods, mistakes of one for the other led to many divergences between the various witnesses to the text. Certain common words were especially liable to confusion, including (1) *'bd*, "serve," and *'br*, "cross over" (Isa. 23:10; Jer.

2:20; 7:29; 15:14; etc.); (2) *'ḥd*, "one," and *'ḥr*, "other" (Gen. 22:13; 43:14; etc.); and (3) *'d(w)m*, "Edom," and *'rm*, "Aram" (1 Sam. 21:8; 22:9; 2 Sam. 8:12–13 [cf. 1 Chron. 18:12]; 2 Kings 16:6; 24:2; Jer 35:11; 2 Chron. 20:2; etc.).

Gen. 10:4	MT	דדנים
	Samaritan	רדנים
1 Chron. 1:7	MT	רדנים

Interpreters of Gen. 10:4 often take MT's "Dodanim" as a mistake for "Rodanim" (i.e., the people of Rhodes), the reading of the Samaritan Pentateuch and LXX *(rhodioi)* in Gen. 10:4 and MT in 1 Chron. 1:7.

Num. 16:15	MT	לא חמור אחד מהם נשאתי
	LXX =	לא חמור אחד מהם נשאתי

Not one *ass/valuable thing* of theirs have I taken!

Isa. 14:4	MT	שבתה מדהבה
	1QIsaᵃ	שבתה מרהבה

The *oppressive(?)*[7]/*boisterous* city is at rest.

Ps. 54:5	MT	כי זרים קמו עלי
	MTᴹˢˢ, Targ.	כי זדים קמו עלי

For *strangers/arrogant men* have arisen against me.

g. ה / ח

2 Sam. 13:37	MT(K)	עמי חור
	MT(Q)	עמיהוד

The variation in this name ("Ammi Hur" or "Ammihud") involves confusion of *dalet* and *reš* (see C.1.f, above) as well as *he* and *ḥet*.

Isa. 19:18	MT	עיר ההרס
	1QIsaᵃ	עיר החרס

The Qumran scroll, along with a number of manuscripts of MT as well as other witnesses, preserves the reading most critics regard as original, *'îr haḥeres*, "the City of the Sun." In MT this became *'îr haheres*, "the City of Destruction." Some critics believe this to have been a deliberate change (cf. D.3., below).

Prov. 9:1	MT	חצבה עמודיה שבעה
	LXX =	הצבה עמודיה שבעה

In this passage we read that Wisdom has built her house, and, according to MT, "she has hewn her seven pillars." Corresponding to *ḥāṣĕbâ*, "has hewn," however, LXX has *kai hypēreisen*, which reflects *hiṣṣîbâ*, "has erected" (cf.

---

7. For this interpretation of *mdhbh*, see H. M. Orlinsky ("*Madhebah* in Isaiah xiv 4," *Vetus Testamentum* 7 [1957]:202–3), who points out that *mrhbh* is the "easier" reading. MT, whatever it means, preserves the primitive text here.

Syr., Targ.). This latter reading was probably original, *ḥṣbh* having become *ḥṣbh* in MT by confusion of *he* and *ḥet*.

h. ו / ז

Ezek. 47:17, 18, 19   MT   ואת

                  MT^{MSS}   זאת

As v. 20 shows, the correct reading in each of these three verses is *z't*, which is preserved in a few manuscripts of MT and certain other witnesses. In the Leningrad Codex and other major manuscripts of MT, this has become *w't* by confusion of *waw* and *zayin*.

Prov. 8:29   MT   בחוקו מוסדי ארץ

            LXX = בחזקו מוסדי ארץ

                    When he *marked off/strengthened* the foundations of the earth

This example shows that graphic confusion might be precipitated by some additional factor. The miscopying of *bḥzqw* as *bḥwqw* in MT was provoked by the scribe's memory of *bḥwqw* in v. 27.

i. ו / י

Isa. 28:10   MT   צו לצו צו לצו

          1QIsa^a   צי לצי צי לצי

Prov. 11:3   MT(K)   וסלף בוגדים ושדם

                    And the deceit of the treacherous *and their destruction [?]*

           MT(Q)   וסלף בוגדים ישדם

                    And the deceit of the treacherous *destroys them.*

The *qĕrê* is supported by the versions.

Prov. 13:20   MT(K)   הלוך את חכמים וחכם

                    Walk with wise men *and be wise!*

           MT(Q)   הלך את חכמים יחכם

                    He who walks with wise men *will become wise.*

The parallel, *wr'h ksylym yrw'*, "But he who associates with fools will come to harm," favors the *qĕrê*.

j. ו / ר

Gen. 49:26   MT   הורי עד

                    those who conceived me to

            LXX = הררי עד

                    the eternal mountains

The obscure reading of MT apparently arose from a scribe's misreading of the first *reš* as *waw*.

1 Sam. 14:47   MT   ובכל אשר יפנה ירשיע

LXX = ובכל אשר יפנה יושיע

And wherever he turned, *he acted wickedly/was victorious.*

Some critics think MT's reading is a consequence of deliberate tampering by a scribe hostile to Saul, but the confusion of *waw* and *reš* is sufficient to explain the change.

Ezek. 32:27   MT   נפלים מערלים

LXX = נפלים מעולם

the fallen ones *of the uncircumcised/of old*

LXX reflects the primitive situation. MT arose by confusion of *waw* and *reš* under the influence of the occurrence of *'rlym* frequently elsewhere in the passage (vv. 19, 21, 24, 25, 26, 28, 29, 30, 32).

k. נ / כ

Josh. 8:13   MT   וילך יהושוע

MTᴹˢˢ   וילן יהושוע

And Joshua *went/spent the night*

Isa. 33:1   MT   כנלתך לבגד יבגדו בך

1QIsaᵃ   ככלתך לבגד יבגדו בך

When *you have* ... *[?]/finished* cheating, someone will cheat you.

Evidently the scroll preserves the primitive text. The unintelligible reading of MT is the result of confusion of *kap* and *nun.*

l. מ / ס

2 Sam. 21:18   MT   סבכי

2 Sam. 23:27   MT   מבני

LXXᴸ = סבני

LXXᴹˢˢ = סבכי

The variation in this name is the result of graphic confusion of *mem* and *samek,* on the one hand, and *kap* and *nun* (cf. C.1.k, above), on the other. Thus *mbny* arose from *sbky* (*sibbĕkay,* "Sibbecai"), which was probably the original form of the name (cf. 1 Chron. 11:29). *Sbny* is either an intermediate form or a partially corrected form.

Isa. 40:6   MT   חסדו   its loyalty

LXX = חמדו [?] its delight

This is a probable, but not certain, example of confusion of *mem* and *samek.* The translation of *ḥmd* by *doxa* is not otherwise attested, and the reading of LXX is actually *doxa anthrōpou,* "the glory of mankind," as if *ḥmd 'dm.* On the other hand, the LXX of Isaiah is frequently paraphrastic and interpretative, and 1 Peter 1:24 preserves the expected *doxa autēs = ḥmdw.*

m. ע / צ

2 Kings 20:4   MT(K)   העיר   the city

MT(Q)   חצר   the court

The versions and many manuscripts of MT support the *qěrê*, but the verse is replete with textual problems.

2. Misdivision

Another common error that did not affect the length of the text was misdivision. A scribe sometimes divided words at the wrong place, attaching one or more of the letters of one word to an adjacent word.

Gen. 49:19–20   MT   ¹⁹ ... הוא יגד עקב²⁰מאשר שמנה לחמו

¹⁹ ... He will raid *at the heel.* ²⁰*More than Asher's,* his food is rich.

versions = ¹⁹ ... הוא יגד עקבם²⁰אשר שמנה לחמו

¹⁹ ... He will raid *at their heel.* ²⁰*As for Asher,* his food is rich.

The error in MT occurred when a scribe attached the *mem* at the end of *'qbm* to the beginning of the following word, *'šr*.

Num. 23:10   MT   מי מנה עפר יעקב

ומספר את רבע ישראל

LXX =   מי מנה עפר יעקב

ומי ספר את רבע ישראל

Who has counted the dust of Jacob

And the number of/And who has numbered the dustcloud of Israel?

The poetic parallel, *my mnh*, "Who has counted," shows the reading of LXX, *wmy spr*, "And who has numbered," to be superior. In MT the word division was omitted and the *mater lectionis (-y)* was lost—thus, *wmspr*, "And the number of."

Jer. 23:33   MT   את מה משא   What burden?

versions = אתם המשא   You are the burden!

The context shows that the reading reflected in the versions is correct. The two words were read as three in MT under the influence of *mh mś'* earlier in the verse.

Hos. 6:5   MT   ומשפטיך אור יצא

And your judgments, light goes forth.

LXX = ומשפטי כאור יצא

And my judgment goes forth like light.

The obscure reading of MT arose when a scribe attached the *k-* of *k'wr* to the preceding word in a text like that reflected by LXX.

49

Amos 6:12   MT   אם יחרוש בבקרים
Does one plow *with oxen?*

emendation   אם יחרוש בבקר ים
Does one plow *the sea with oxen?*

The second reading, which seems to have been suggested first by J. D. Michaelis, is not represented among the ancient witnesses to the text. Nevertheless, it is preferred by many modern critics. It suits the parallelism of the verse, following *hyrṣwn bsl' swsym*, "Do horses run upon the rock?" MT may reflect grammatical modernizing (see C.4, below): The plural *bqrym*, "oxen," occurs elsewhere only in 2 Chron. 4:3, where the text is suspect (cf. 1 Kings 7:24), and Neh. 10:37 (*bqrynw*), and we expect the collective *bqr*, "oxen," in Amos.

3. Transposition (Metathesis)

Transposition, or metathesis, refers to an exchange of the positions of consonants within a word. It occurs in Hebrew as a regular grammatical phenomenon (e.g., the exchange of *taw* and a sibilant in *Hitpaʻel* verbs: *hištammēr* for *hitšammēr*) and as a lexical phenomenon, as in the following example.

Lev. 3:7   MT   כשב
MTTMSS   כבש

Biblical Hebrew shows lexical variation between *kśb* (Lev. 3:7; 4:35; 7:23; etc.) and *kbś* (Lev. 4:32; 12:6; etc.), both "lamb," and the scribes occasionally substituted one of these forms for the other.

Whether grammatical or lexical, however, transposition as a regular feature of the language is of less concern to the textual critic than transposition as a form of textual accident. Scribes sometimes reversed the order of letters within words by accident when copying the text.

Deut. 31:1   MT   וילך משה וידבר את הדברים האלה
And Moses *went* and spoke these words.

4QDtn   ויכל משה וידבר את הדברים האלה
And Moses *finished* speaking these words.

In this example, a scribe miscopied *wykl* as *wylk*, reversing the order of *kap* and *lamed*. The reading of the Qumran scroll, also reflected by LXX, is superior (cf. Deut. 32:45 [MT]).

1 Sam. 14:27   MT(K)   ותראנה עיניו
MT(Q)   ותארנה עיניו
And his eyes *saw/brightened.*

The *qěrê*, which is clearly superior, is supported by the versions.

Ezek. 36:14   MT(K)   וגויך לא תכשלי עוד
MT(Q)   וגויך לא תשכלי עוד
You shall no longer *totter/bereave* your nation.

50

Though the *ketîb* is repeated in v. 15, probably as a displaced dittograph (cf. the discussion in A.2.b, above), the *qĕrê* better suits the parallel ("you shall no longer devour men") and is more likely to have been original.

Ps. 49:12   MT   קרבם בתימו לעולם

versions = קבר(י)ם בתימו לעולם

Their insides [?]/graves are their houses forever.

The obscure reading of MT arose from transposition of *bet* and *reš*.

4. Modernization

Because the biblical writings derive from several different time periods, they display a variety of early and late linguistic features. The archaic components of the language, however, were not always recognized by the scribes, who were most familiar with the latest form of the language. In the course of the transmission of the text, therefore, archaic features were often removed by conscious or unconscious modernization. Spelling was modified to bring it in line with the orthographic practices most familiar to the scribe or to reflect current pronunciation. Grammatical archaisms were eliminated or reinterpreted.

a. Grammar

Scribes frequently modernized archaic features of the grammar of a passage. Thus, for example, a comparison of synoptic passages in Kings and Chronicles will show that imperfect plural verbs with the archaic *-ûn* ending (the so-called paragogic *nun*) in Kings often lack the *-n* in Chronicles (1 Kings 8:38, 43 = 2 Chron. 6:29, 33; 1 Kings 12:24 = 2 Chron. 11:4; 2 Kings 11:5 = 2 Chron. 23:4).

In cases where archaic features were retained, they were sometimes misunderstood by the scribes, and this led to various kinds of textual corruption. The following examples are chosen to illustrate two grammatical archaisms that frequently confused the scribes.

(1) The long form of prepositions. In Biblical Hebrew there are long forms of certain common prepositions: *bĕmô* for *bĕ-*, *kĕmô* for *kĕ-*, and *lĕmô* for *lĕ-*. These forms occur occasionally in poetry and rarely in prose. They were not familiar to the scribes, who frequently misunderstood them, as the following examples show.

1 Sam. 4:8   MT   במדבר

in the wilderness

LXX = ובמדבר

and in the wilderness

As the text is understood in both of these witnesses, the Egyptians were stricken with scourges "in the wilderness," which is contrary to biblical

51

tradition. LXX reflects the primitive text in archaic orthography. Read °*ûbĕmō deber*, "and with pestilence."

1 Sam. 10:27 (11:1) MT ויהי כמחריש

and he was like someone who keeps silent

4QSam[a] ויהי כמו חדש

And about a month later

The reading of the scroll is supported by LXX. The corruption in MT was the result of a scribe's failure to recognize the long form of the preposition. Note also the confusion of *dalet* and *reš* (cf. C.1.f, above).

Ps. 11:1   MT(Q) נודי הרכם צפור

         LXX = נודי הר כמו צפור

Flee to the mountain like a bird!

MT (which can hardly mean "Flee to your mountain, O bird!") makes no sense. It arose from a text like that of the *Vorlage* of LXX when a scribe mistook the preposition *km(w)* for a suffix and attached it to the preceding word. (Note the secondary corruption in MT[K], where the verb has become plural *[nwdw]* under the influence of *hrkm*, "your [plural] mountain.")

(2) Enclitic mem. After the discovery of the Ugaritic poetry, scholars became aware of the presence of enclitic *mem* in Biblical Hebrew. The scribes seem to have been altogether unaware of the phenomenon, which caused textual confusion wherever it survived. The following examples are representative.

Deut. 33:11   MT מחץ מתנים קמיו

     Samaritan מחץ מתני קמיו

Smash the loins of his adversaries!

The original reading was *mtny-m*, the dual construct with enclitic *mem*. The *-m*, however, bewildered the scribes, who were forced either to strike it, as they did in the Samaritan Pentateuch, or read *mtnym* as a very awkward absolute.

2 Sam. 22:16   אפיקי ים

Ps. 18:16   אפיקי מים

Again the scribes' confusion by a noun followed by enclitic *mem* has been resolved in two ways. In 2 Sam. 22:16 the meaning of the original '*pyqy-m ym*, "the channels of the sea," was preserved by striking the *mem*. In Ps. 18:16 the *mem* was grouped with the following word—thus, "the channels of the *water*."

Ps. 29:6   MT   וירקידם כמו עגל

                           לבנון ושרין כמו בן ראמים

And he causes them[8] to skip like a calf,

Lebanon and Sirion like the young of wild oxes.

8. Namely, the cedars of Lebanon (cf. v. 5).

emendation   וירקיד־ם כמו עגל לבנון
ושריון כמו בן ראם־ם

And he causes Lebanon to skip like a calf,
And Sirion like the young of a wild ox.

Recognition of the enclitic *mems* removes the difficulties of MT and restores the poetic symmetry of the verse.

b. Spelling

In order to identify textual problems caused by changing spelling practices, the critic must be familiar with the history of Hebrew orthography. Generally speaking, the earliest, purely consonantal spelling gave way gradually to a fuller orthography, that is, one in which *matres lectionis* were used, first to indicate final long vowels and subsequently to indicate vowels in medial positions. Within the Bible itself there is considerable orthographic variety. The orthography of Ezra-Nehemiah-Chronicles, for example, is generally fuller than that of the other books. The scribes who copied the manuscripts in postbiblical times were accustomed to a spelling system that was very full in comparison to most of the biblical texts, and they sometimes updated the spelling in words or passages they copied. The orthography of 1QIsa[a], for example, is much fuller than that of Isaiah in MT.

Such orthographic modernization usually did not produce results that require text-critical analysis. That is, the critic will often deem a discrepancy between readings that is "purely orthographic" to be insignificant. Sometimes, however, a word written in the older, defective orthography was open to more than one interpretation, and this ambiguity gave rise to significantly different readings when the spelling was modernized in the various witnesses to reflect divergent understandings of the text. This process is illustrated by the following examples.

Ps. 84:7   MT   ישיתהו
they make it

MT[MSS]   ישיתהו
he appoints it

MT[MSS]   ישתהו
he drinks it

MT[MSS]   ישתוהו
they drink it

In this extreme example an original reading in defective orthography, °*yšthw*, was interpreted in four different ways, namely, *yĕšîtûhû* by the Leningrad Codex, *yĕšîtēhû* by other manuscripts of MT and by LXX, *yištēhû* by other manuscripts of MT, and *yištûhû* by still other manuscripts of MT.

53

Isa. 24:23   וחפרה הלבנה ובושה החמה

MT   Then *the moon* will blush and *the sun* will be ashamed.

LXX = Then *the brick* will blush and *the wall* will be ashamed.

In this case there is no difference between the text of MT and that of the *Vorlage* of LXX. There is, however, a considerable difference between the interpretations of the shared text made in the two traditions. This difference arose from the ambiguity of *ḥḥmh* in the older orthography. In MT this was read *haḥammâ*, "the sun," and the parallel, *ḥlbnh*, was understood as *hallĕbānâ*, "the moon." In LXX, however, *ḥḥmh* was interpreted as *haḥōmâ*, "the wall," and the parallel read *hallĕbēnâ*, "the brick." Note that in the later orthography this ambiguity would have been eliminated by the fuller spelling *ḥḥwmh = haḥômâ*, "the wall."

In addition to the gradual introduction of fuller spelling, other changes took place during the development of Hebrew orthography. The following example shows how one of these changes led to confusion in the text.

2 Sam. 21:1   MT   ויאמר יהוה אל שאול ואל בית הדמים

And Yahweh said, "Upon Saul and upon a house is the bloodguilt . . ."

emendation   ויאמר יהוה על שאול ועל ביתה דמים

And Yahweh said, "There is bloodguilt upon Saul and upon his house . . ."

MT's misdivision of *byth dmym* (cf. LXX) was the result of a scribe's misinterpretation of *-h* in *bêtô*. The use of *he* as a marker for final *ô* was once a standard practice, but it survives only as an archaism in the orthography of the Bible, where *waw* ordinarily indicates final *ô*.

c. Pronunciation

Finally we note that the various witnesses to the biblical text display numerous divergent readings that arose from scribal adjustment of the text to reflect the changing pronunciation of the language. The examples that follow are grouped according to certain pronunciation changes of special importance for textual criticism.

(1) Quiescence of 'alep. In the course of the development of the language the pronunciation of *'alep* weakened, until it was silent in certain positions. As a result, there are many words in the Hebrew Bible in which no *'alep* is found in a place it is expected.

Num. 11:11   MT   מצתי
  Samaritan   מצאתי
1 Sam. 1:17   MT   שלתך
  MT^{MSS}   שאלתך

Job 1:21   MT(K)   יצתי
             MT(Q)   יצאתי

Quiescence of 'alep is of most concern to the textual critic when it has led to some kind of confusion in one or more of the ancient witnesses, as in the following case.

Jer. 22:23   MT   מה נחנת
                    How you will be pitied!

             LXX = מה נאנחת
                    How you will groan!

The primitive text was that represented by LXX. With quiescence of 'alep, the verb was spelled °nnḥt, which became nḥnt in MT by metathesis (C.3, above).

(2) Quiescence of 'ayin. 'Ayin was a stronger consonant than 'alep, and there is little evidence in the biblical text for quiescence of 'ayin comparable to the sporadic but widespread loss of 'alep. Nevertheless, that 'ayin weakened to the point of quiescence in the postbiblical period is shown by the following readings from the great Qumran Isaiah scroll (1QIsaᵃ). In each of these three cases the scribe omitted 'ayin when he copied his text but subsequently corrected the words by adding the letter above the line.

Isa. 1:1   MT   ישעיהו
             1QIsaᵃ   ישׁיהו [with supralinear ע]
Isa. 5:21   MT   בעיניהם
             1QIsaᵃ   ביניהם [with supralinear ע]
Isa. 9:7   MT   יעקוב
             1QIsaᵃ   יקוב [with supralinear ע]

Within MT itself there are certain place-names spelled alternatively with and without 'ayin.

Josh. 15:50   אשתמה
Josh. 21:14   אשתמע
                     Eshtemoa
Josh. 19:3   בלה
Josh. 15:29   בעלה
                     Baalah

Such examples suggest that quiescence of 'ayin might account for divergent readings in cases such as the following:

Ps. 28:8   MT   יהוה עז למו
          versions = יהוה עז לעמו

Surely the intended meaning was "Yahweh is a stronghold *to his people.*" At a time when the 'ayin was not pronounced, however, a scribe copied l'mw as lmw, which is now interpreted in MT as lāmô, as if "to himself."

Amos 8:8   MT(K)   ונשקה
             MT(Q)   ונשקעה

The reading of the *qěrê* (*wĕnišqě'â*, "and it will subside") must be original. The *kĕtîb* arose at a time when the *'ayin* was not pronounced. Note that in MT the verb is preceded by another (*wngršh*, "and it will be driven away"), which probably arose as a replacement after the loss of the *'ayin* rendered the original verb obscure; it is missing in LXX and one manuscript of MT. Both verbs are preserved in the conflate text of the Leningrad Codex.

5. Prosaizing

The scribes tended to adjust poetry to the grammatical and syntactical conventions of prose.

a. Insertion of Copulatives

Hebrew poetry used relative particles and conjunctions (*wĕ-*, *'ăšer*, *kî*, etc.) sparingly in comparison to Hebrew prose, but the ancient witnesses to many poetic texts show their introduction by scribes.

Eccl. 6:1   MT   יש רעה אשר ראיתי תחת השמש

                MTᴹˢˢ   יש רעה   ראיתי תחת השמש

There is an evil that I have seen under the sun.

Compare also Eccl. 5:12. A scribe inserted *'ăšer* where it would have been expected in the prose idiom.[9]

Ps. 31:22   MT   ברוך יהוה כי הפליא חסדו

            MTᴹˢˢ   ברוך יהוה אשר הפליא חסדו

Blessed be Yahweh, *because he/who* has wondrously shown his loyalty!

The variation between *'ăšer* and *kî* in various manuscripts of MT shows that the original text had neither.

b. Insertion of 't.

The accusative particle *'ēt*, which was characteristic of Hebrew prose, was used rarely or never in all but the latest biblical poetry. Occasionally, however, the scribes inserted it into poetic passages in places where it would have been expected in prose.

Ps. 105:11   לך אתן את ארץ כנען

1 Chron. 16:18   לך אתן   ארץ כנען

To you I will give the land of Canaan.

c. Insertion of the Article

The use of the definite article was much more restricted in poetry than in

---

9. Some may argue that Eccl. 6:1 *is* prose, so that it is improper to speak of the introduction of *'ăšer* as "prosaizing." Prose or not, however, the passage shares the lyrical quality that characterizes most of the book, and this quality is diminished by the introduction of prose particles.

prose, but the scribes often supplied it in poetic passages where it was lacking.

Judg. 5:21   MT   מן שמים

            MT^MSS מן השמים

                  from the sky

6. Interpretative Errors

Certain textual problems lie on the boundary of the textual critic's domain. Among these are problems that involve changes not to the consonantal text but to the interpretative framework in which it has been transmitted.

a. Misdivision of Verses

Sometimes the misdivision of a word caused a misdivision between verses (cf. the example of Gen. 49:19–20, cited above in C.2). In other cases, however, verses were misdivided as a result of a misinterpretation of the meaning of the passage as a whole or a misunderstanding of its poetic form. Note the following example.

Joel 2:1–2   ¹ . . . כי בא יום יהוה כי קרוב ²יום חשך ואפלה

          MT   ¹ . . . For the day of Yahweh is coming, for it is near. ²A day of darkness and gloom . . .

          Syriac ² . . . For the day of Yahweh is coming. ²For a day of darkness and gloom is near . . .

The arrangement of the Peshiṭta is metrically preferable.

b. Misvocalization

Often the same consonantal text is interpreted in different ways by the various witnesses, as shown by the vocalization of MT or the translation of one of the versions. The kind of ambiguity that led to this variety was most likely to exist in words written in the archaic, "defective" orthography (cf. the example of Isa. 24:23 in C.4.b, above), but as the following example shows, it was not confined to such cases.

Isa. 7:11   העמק שאלה או הגבה למעלה

          MT   whether it is deep—ask!—or as high as the sky

       versions   whether it is as deep as Sheol or as high as the sky

MT's treatment of *š'lh* as an imperative, *šĕ'ālâ*, "ask!" is very awkward. The versions understand it correctly as *šĕ'ōlāh*, "(toward) Sheol."

D. DELIBERATE CHANGES

Most of the examples of textual change listed above occurred without the knowledge or intention of the scribes. The rest were intentional changes made for the purpose of clarifying the text (glosses, explicitation, etc.). In none of these cases did a scribe intend to alter the meaning of the text as he understood it. There are, however, a few places in the Hebrew Bible where deliberate changes of the latter kind do seem to have taken place. That is, there are a few places where the scribes seem to have made changes with the intent to alter the meaning of the passage.

1. *The* tiqqûnê sôpĕrîm

One group of scribal alterations involved the change of one or a few letters in order to disguise the meaning of the text. The purpose was euphemistic. The scribes wanted to protect God or some highly revered human figure from injury or reproach. The Massoretes, who were aware of these euphemistic changes, called them *tiqqûnê sôpĕrîm*, "emendations of the scribes," of which they compiled a list of eighteen.[10] The first two of the following examples are taken from the Massoretic list.

1 Sam. 3:13 MT כי מקללים להם בניו
that his sons were blaspheming *for themselves*
LXX = כי מקללים אלהים בניו
that his sons were blaspheming *God*

MT seems to have been deliberately altered by a scribe who wanted to remove the dishonor to God expressed by the original text as preserved in LXX.

Job 7:20 MT ואהיה עלי למשא
And I have become a burden *to myself.*
versions = ואהיה עליך למשא
And I have become a burden *to you.*

Evidently the suggestion that Job had become a burden to God was regarded as impious or blasphemous by a scribe, who altered *'lyk,* which is reflected in the versions, to *'ly.*

1 Kings 9:8 MT והבית הזה יהיה עליון
And this house will become *most high.*
versions = והבית הזה יהיה לעיין
And this house will become *ruins.*

Although this emendation does not appear in the Massoretic list of eighteen, it appears to be of the same type. A scribe changed *l'yyn* to *'lywn* to protect the dignity of the temple.

Deut. 32:8 MT יצב גבלת עמים למספר בני ישראל
4QDtq יצב גבלת עמים למספר בני האלהים

10. The Massoretic list seems to be neither complete nor accurate. It omits many passages that probably contain authentic emendations, and it includes several that probably do not. On this subject in general, see the excellent study of C. McCarthy, *The Tiqqune Sopherim and Other Theological Corrections in the Masoretic Text of the Old Testament* (Orbis Biblicus et Orientalis 36; Göttingen: Vandenhoeck & Ruprecht, 1981).

He established the boundaries of the peoples
according to the number of the sons of *Israel/God.*
The reading of the scroll is confirmed by LXX and other versions. The
original can be taken to mean that Yahweh was one of the sons of God to
whom Elyon parceled out peoples. The alteration of *h'lhym* (or perhaps '*l* or
'*lym*) to *yśr'l* suppressed this interpretation.

2. Euphemistic Insertions

The scribes sometimes added words to the text to avoid dishonor to God or
revered persons. The purpose of these insertions, then, was the same as that
of the *tiqqûnê sôpěrîm.*

2 Sam. 12:9   LXX^L = יהוה   מדוע בזית את

           MT   מדוע בזית את דבר יהוה

Why do you treat *Yahweh/the word of Yahweh*
with contempt?

A scribe softened the insult to Yahweh by inserting *dbr.* The shorter, original
text is reflected in the so-called Lucianic manuscripts of LXX and Theodotion (cf. Old Latin).

2 Sam. 12:14   MT   נאץ נאצת את איבי יהוה

You have insulted *the enemies of Yahweh.*

     4QSam^a   [נ[אץ נאצ[ת] את [ד]בר יהוה

You have insulted *the word of Yahweh.*

    LXX^MS = יהוה   נאץ נאצת את

You have insulted *Yahweh.*

The third reading is reflected only in one Greek minuscule. Nevertheless,
the fact that MT and the Qumran scroll have *different* euphemistic
insertions shows that the primitive text read '*t yhwh.*

1 Sam. 25:22   LXX = לדוד   כה יעשה אלהים

           MT   כה יעשה אלהים לאיבי דוד

May God do thus *to David/to the enemies of
David!*

In this case the purpose of the euphemistic insertion was to protect David
from the effects of the curse. Cf. 1 Sam. 20:16.

Judg. 18:30   MT^MSS   יהונתן בן גרשם בן משה

           MT   יהונתן בן גרשם בן מישה

Jonathan, son of Gershom, son of *Moses/
Manasseh.*

This belongs to a small group of passages containing what the Massoretes
called '*ôtiyyôt tělôyôt,* "suspended letters." The *nun* was inserted above the
line in order to change "Moses" to "Manasseh," thereby removing Moses'
name from the scandalous context. The original reading was preserved in a
few manuscripts of MT as well as LXX and the Vulgate.

3. Euphemistic Substitutions

When an existing reading was deemed theologically unacceptable by a scribe, it was sometimes replaced. This can be illustrated by two examples or groups of examples.

Consider first the widespread substitution of the word *bōšet*, "shame," for the divine name *ba'al*, "Baal." Many scribes seem to have considered *ba'al* an abomination that should not appear in the biblical text. Its replacement with *bōšet* is most familiar in names of the early monarchical period that contained *ba'al* as a theophorous element, as in the following case.

2 Sam. 2:8; etc.   MT   איש בשת   Ishbosheth

   MXX MS = איש בעל   Ishbaal

Cf. 1 Chron. 8:33; 9:39.

But the same substitution was made elsewhere in passages where *ba'al* stood independently.

1 Kings 18:19, 25   MT   הבעל

   LXX   τῆς αἰσχύνης = הבשת

Jer. 11:13   MT   לבשת

   LXX   τῇ βααλ = לבעל

Second, note the euphemistic replacement of words of cursing with words of blessing in two groups of passages where God is the object, (a) 1 Kings 21:10, 13 and (b) Job 1:5, 11 and 2:5, 9. In these cases, however, there is no support among extant witnesses for the presumed original, non-euphemistic reading, and some scholars believe these are euphemisms of the authors, not of the scribes.[11]

4. Harmonizing Substitutions

Critics have noticed a few passages in which the scribes seem to have deliberately substituted one reading for another in order to remove problems of interpretation from the text. The following passage is often cited to illustrate this phenomenon.

Gen. 2:2   MT   ויכל אלהים ביום השביעי מלאכתו

   Samaritan   ויכל אלהים ביום הששי מלאכתו

   And God completed his work on the *seventh/sixth* day.

The reading of the Samaritan Pentateuch is shared by LXX and the Peshiṭta. It came from the hand of a scribe who thought the original reading, preserved in MT, was erroneous.

---

11. See McCarthy, *Tiqqune Sopherim*, 191–95.

5. Suppressed Readings

In a few instances the scribes seem to have suppressed corrupt readings in preference to either altering the text or reproducing an obvious error.

1 Sam. 13:1   MT   בן שנה שאול במלכו ושתי שנים מלך על ישראל

Saul was a year old [?] when he began to reign, and he reigned two years over Israel.

LXX^B   . . .

The numbers in the reading of MT are obviously incorrect. In the tradition behind the Codex Vaticanus the entire verse was suppressed to avoid perpetuating the error.

2 Sam. 3:7   LXX^BL   μεμφιβοσθε υἱὸς σαουλ

MT   . . .

In this case it is MT that suppresses an obvious error. Ishbosheth, not Mephibosheth, is the son of Saul involved in the events recounted in this chapter. In the major manuscripts of MT, which originally shared the mistake of LXX, the name *mpybšt* was excised; in a few manuscripts it was corrected to *'yš bšt*.

III

The Basic Procedures of Textual Criticism

When the scholar has acquired an understanding of the goals and methods of textual criticism (Chapter I) and a familiarity with the characteristic types of textual corruption (Chapter II), he is ready to begin the work of textual repair. Specifically, then, what does he do? How does he approach his task?

This chapter describes the process of textual criticism. It presents the method by which the critic establishes the text of a biblical passage. It sets out the procedures he follows in evaluating the various witnesses to the passage and, where divergences exist, choosing between readings.

A. THE THREE STAGES OF TEXTUAL CRITICISM

The process of textual criticism, as practiced by scholars in various literary fields, is usually said to have three parts or stages. Traditionally, these are called *recensio, examinatio,* and *emendatio.*

Recensio refers to the preliminary sorting of the various witnesses to determine their relative worth. The critic gathers the witnesses, compares them *(collatio)*, and attempts to determine the relationships among them. He asks which is descended from which and tries to establish a "family tree of manuscripts" *(stemma codicum)*. Most especially, he endeavors to identify manuscripts that are derived entirely from others; they have no independent value and can be excluded from consideration *(eliminatio codicum descriptorum,* "the elimination of derivative manuscripts"). The goal of *recensio*, then, is the isolation of those witnesses that, being independent, have a potential claim to originality. In the best case there is only one of these.

Examinatio is the next stage. The critic examines the witnesses isolated by *recensio* to determine which, if any, is primitive.

Emendatio is the final stage. If the critic concludes from his examination of the witnesses that the primitive text has not survived, he attempts to reconstruct it. This stage is sometimes called *divinatio.*

In practice these three stages are seldom entirely distinct, and the critical process is not as straightforward as the scheme suggests. *Recensio* and *examinatio*, for example, very often merge into a single activity by which the original form of the text is identified. *Emendatio* is not often necessary, and when it is, the critic's intuition may present him with the solution early in his work rather than at the end. The entire process, moreover, must be adjusted to the peculiarities of every type of text and textual tradition— *recensio* of the witnesses to the *Iliad* is very different from that of the folios and quartos of *Twelfth Night* (for example) or the manuscripts of Whitman's "Leaves of Grass"—and this is especially true for the text of the Hebrew Bible. Nevertheless, biblical textual criticism follows roughly the process just outlined.

B. THE CRITICAL PROCESS

The biblical textual critic begins by evaluating the available witnesses to determine the relationships among them. It is not customary among biblical scholars to use the term *recensio* for this evaluation, perhaps because of the danger of confusion involving the word "recension," which refers to a revision of one witness to a text toward another and, in our field, especially to the revision of the Septuagint toward the developing rabbinic Bible tradition in antiquity. Thus we are safer referring to the first stage of the critical process as "the evaluation of witnesses."

Next the critic analyzes the witnesses identified by this evaluation in an attempt to determine which, if any, is primitive. This is the stage of *examinatio*, but in the biblical field it usually involves a comparison of several texts rather than a critical examination of one. That is, it is usually a matter of "choosing between readings."

When the biblical textual critic believes that none of the transmitted readings is primitive, he attempts to reconstruct the primitive text. This is *emendatio*, and here we retain the traditional term, "emendation."

1. The Evaluation of Witnesses

The purpose of the evaluation is to certify the independence, authenticity, and retrovertibility of the various witnesses. The criterion of independence is one that is always applied in the initial stages of the critical process, as we have seen. Witnesses derived entirely from other witnesses and lacking independent value are excluded. The criteria of authenticity and retrovertibility, on the other hand, are peculiar to the criticism of the Hebrew Bible. Because many of the witnesses to the biblical text are not in the original language of the text, each of them must be evaluated to determine whether it offers genuine and unambiguous evidence of a Hebrew reading. As explained below, non-Hebrew readings that seem

63

independent are sometimes no more than translational variants of known readings. Such readings are excluded by the criterion of authenticity. In other cases the translation is so free or paraphrastic that the Hebrew original cannot be determined. Readings that cannot be converted into Hebrew are excluded by the criterion of retrovertibility.

It follows that this first stage in biblical textual criticism is generally an evaluation of the *non-Hebrew* witnesses to the text. Although there are cases where one Hebrew manuscript can be shown to derive from another, MT and other Hebrew witnesses (the Samaritan Pentateuch and the various Qumran manuscripts) are not susceptible to the criteria of authenticity and retrovertibility, as we have described them. At the beginning of his work, therefore, the critic is chiefly concerned with the non-Hebrew witnesses to the text of a given passage. He attempts to identify those that may be set alongside the Hebrew witnesses with a claim to possible originality.

If no non-Hebrew witness qualifies and if there are no non-Massoretic Hebrew witnesses, the critic's work is usually finished when this preliminary evaluation is complete. Since the reading of MT is the only one with sound textual support, the critic will adopt it, unless he decides to propose an emendation. Often, however, one non-Massoretic witness (Hebrew or otherwise) and sometimes two or more will be identified as possibly original (independent and authentic), and if any of the readings reflected by these witnesses diverges from that of MT, the procedures listed below for choosing between divergent readings will be followed.

a. Evaluative Criteria

Each non-Hebrew witness is evaluated according to the following criteria.

(1) Independence. A reading that is derived from, adjusted to, or otherwise dependent on another reading is of only secondary value to the critic. There are at least three types of textual dependence: (1) dependence of a manuscript in a given language on another in the same language, such as the dependence of one of the minor Greek manuscripts (minuscules or cursives) on one of the great uncials; (2) dependence of a manuscript in one language on one in another (usually LXX), such as the dependence of the Old Latin on LXX; and (3) dependence of a non-Hebrew manuscript on MT, such as the dependence of the Targum on MT. Also included in the second and third categories are those cases where a manuscript is dependent on LXX or MT because of recensional activity—cases, in other words, where the text of a manuscript has been secondarily adjusted to conform to that of LXX, as in the case of the Vulgate, or MT, as in the case of the Hexaplaric text of LXX.

The critic identifies those witnesses that lack independent value and excludes them from consideration. Note, however, that he must do this *for each reading individually*. A witness that is usually derivative and valueless may preserve an independent reading in a given case. The general rule that applies is this: When witness B is known to be dependent upon witness A, the value of B is discounted *when it agrees with A*. The corollary, however, is this: When B *disagrees* with A, it may reflect an independent and authentic reading, which must then be considered as possibly original. The following example illustrates this point.

2 Sam. 12:21   MT   בעבור הילד חי

> for the sake of the child (when) alive

LXX^L ἔτι (γαρ) τοῦ παιδίου ζῶντος

= בעוד הילד חי

> while the child was still alive

Syriac כד חי הוא טליא [= LXX^L]

Targum עד דרביא קיים [= LXX^L]

Because both the Peshitta and the Targum ordinarily agree with MT, they are most useful to the critic when they diverge from MT, as in this case. Their agreement here with LXX^L suggests that MT, too, once shared the reading *b'wd* and that *b'bwr* arose secondarily in the developing MT tradition (cf. Chapter II.C.1.f). The other Greek witnesses to this passage are in general agreement with MT, showing that they were revised toward the secondary MT reading; the text of LXX^L is the Old Greek.

(2) *Authenticity*. When one of the ancient translations reflects a reading that is different from that of MT, the critic is usually justified in regarding the reading as authentic and comparing it to that of MT in order to determine which was original. Sometimes, however, there is reason to suspect that a translator improved or corrected a text identical to MT in the process of translation. In such a case the divergent reading is obviously of no value to the critic in his attempt to recover the original text. Consider the following example.

2 Sam. 8:18   MT   ובני דוד כהנים היו

> And the sons of David were priests.

The surprising designation of David's sons as priests finds textual support only in Aquila *(hiereis ēsan)* and the Vulgate *(sacerdotes erant)*. Other versions have *aularchai*, "princes of the court" (LXX), *rwrbyn*, "great men" (Peshitta), and *rbrbyn*, also "great men" (Targum). Should these readings be retroverted as one or more variants to be compared with *khnym*, "priests"? Most critics of the passage have thought not, regarding it more likely that the apparent variants arose as interpretations of *khnym* by translators who believed it impossible that there were non-Levitical priests in the time of David. Note, however, the Chronicler's reading.

1 Chron. 18:17   MT   ‏ובני דוד הראשנים ליד המלך‎

And the sons of David were foremost, next to the king.

In this case the Hebrew text itself seems to have been altered from an original reading like that of MT in 2 Sam. 8:18. This shows that we cannot be sure that LXX *aularchai* is a rendering of *khnym* and not of some other, previously altered Hebrew original.

The example of 2 Sam. 8:18 = 1 Chron. 18:17 illustrates a common problem for the critic. When do apparent divergences in the versions reflect authentic alternative readings and when are they translational? This question can be answered only on the basis of a thorough familiarity with the character of a particular translation in a given book or part of a book. Is the translation usually a literal one, or does it tend to paraphrase? Some preliminary answers to this question are provided in Appendix C.

Sometimes known idiosyncracies in the translation of a particular book provide clues, as in the following example.

Isa. 33:20   MT   ‏חזה ציון קרית מועדנו‎

LXX   ἰδοὺ Σιων ἡ πόλις τὸ σωτήριον ἡμῶν

Behold Zion, the city of our *assembly/salvation!*

We might suppose that *to sōtērion hēmōn* reflects an alternative to *mwʻdnw*, such as *yšwʻtnw*. A familiarity with the LXX of Isaiah, however, shows that this may not be the case. *To sōtērion*, "salvation," appears in correspondence to unlikely equivalents in other passages.

Isa. 38:11   MT   ‏לא אראה יה יה‎

LXX   οὐκέτι μὴ ἴδω τὸ σωτήριον τοῦ θεοῦ

I shall not see *Yahweh [?]/the salvation of God.*

Isa. 40:5   MT   ‏וראו כל בשר יחדו‎

LXX   καὶ ὄψεται πᾶσα σὰρξ τὸ σωτήριον τοῦ θεοῦ

And all flesh will see *together/the salvation of God.*

Isa. 60:6   MT   ‏ותהלת יהוה יבשרו‎

LXX   καὶ τὸ σωτήριον κυρίου εὐαγγελιοῦνται

And they shall broadcast *the praises of Yahweh/ the salvation of the Lord.*

Thus *to sōtērion hēmōn* in Isa. 33:20 cannot be considered authentic evidence of an alternative reading to MT *mwʻdnw*.

(3) Retrovertibility. Retrovertibility refers to the possibility of retroverting a reading into Hebrew. There are many cases in which the Hebrew presupposed by a reading in one of the non-Hebrew witnesses cannot be determined. This unfortunate situation is common in some witnesses, uncommon in others; it is often encountered in certain books of the Bible,

sporadically or rarely in others. It is characteristic of passages of para-phrasing translation in LXX, Targumic passages filled with theological or explicating expansions, and, in short, any passage in one of the ancient translations where confident retroversion into Hebrew is impossible. When this kind of ambiguity exists, the reading in question must be excluded from consideration, even if the critic suspects it contains the primitive text.

Notice that this is a different kind of criterion from the other two just discussed. We have seen that the value of a witness is discounted if it is derivative or inauthentic. Such an exclusion points in a positive direction toward the solution to a textual problem; it simplifies the problem by eliminating one option. But now we see that the value of a witness is discounted if its evidence is ambiguous. An exclusion of this kind is an admission of limitations. When any witness is discarded because its evidence is unclear, rather than because its evidence is positively determined to be without value, the probability of success in solving the textual problem in question is reduced.

b. Evaluative Procedures

The above criteria are applied to the evidence using the following procedures.

(1) Marshal all witnesses. The critic begins by gathering the extant witnesses to the text of his passage. This by itself can be a formidable task. For a given passage a very large number of major and minor witnesses may exist, including numerous manuscript variants within individual witnesses. Fortunately, however, tools are available that provide reliable shortcuts. For most text-critical work, *BHS* is an ample resource for manuscript variants of MT. With regard to the versions, however, the citations in *BHS* are inade-quate for detailed textual study, and the critic will want to turn to other resources. We now have complete or partially complete critical editions of the major non-Hebrew witnesses—the Septuagint, the Peshiṭta, the Tar-gums, and the Vulgate—and of the Samaritan Pentateuch. These are listed in Appendix B. The critic can safely depend upon them for the identifi-cation of important manuscript variants. The critical editions of the Sep-tuagint are also generally reliable sources for variants in the so-called daughter translations of LXX, including the Old Latin, Coptic, Ethiopic, and Syro-Hexapla, as well as early citations of LXX by postbiblical Jewish and Christian writers.

It follows from all of this that the critic can set to work when he has the following on his desk: (1) *BHS*, and critical editions of (2) the Septuagint, (3) the Peshiṭta, (4) the Targum, (5) the Vulgate, and—if he is working in the Pentateuch—(6) the Samaritan Pentateuch. He can expect to reconstruct from these all the important readings reflected in the various witnesses. Of this list, items (1), (2), and, where applicable, (6) are obviously of first importance, since the texts of the Peshiṭta and the Targums are generally close to MT, and the Vulgate seldom provides independent testimony.

In cases where manuscripts from Qumran and other sites contain portions of the text under examination, the critic may find the task of assembling the witnesses somewhat more complicated. Some of these manuscripts are still unpublished, and the places of publication of the others are diverse. Appendix B provides publication information on biblical manuscript discoveries.

(2) Collate the witnesses by language groups. The various witnesses are first compared to others in the same language in order to discover the patterns of divergence or interdependence within a given version. By this process the critic reduces the number of readings that must be considered. It will often be possible, for example, to assign the several Greek witnesses to groups representing only two readings.

(3) Compare LXX and its daughter translations. The critic notes any divergence in the versions of LXX—especially Old Latin, Coptic, Ethiopic, and the Syro-Hexapla—from the reading(s) of LXX itself. Ordinarily the apparatus of one of the critical editions of LXX can be relied upon for this information. Most often the readings of the daughter translations will correspond to one of the Greek readings determined in step 2.

(4) Compare MT and its non-Greek versions. The texts of the Peshiṭta, Targum, and Vulgate are compared to that of MT and divergences noted.

Note that with regard to these three versions we are anticipating subsequent steps here in step 4. The comparison of the Peshiṭta to MT, for example, implies a retroversion of the Syriac into Hebrew (cf. step 5), and the purpose of the comparison is to exclude the Peshiṭta from consideration when it has no independent value (cf. steps 5 and 6). These three versions follow MT so closely, however, that much time can be saved by this preliminary comparison in advance of a full and formal retroversion into Hebrew.

(5) Retrovert into Hebrew. The following readings are now retroverted, that is, translated back from their present language into Hebrew: (1) as many LXX readings as remain after the completion of step 2 above, (2) the reading of any daughter translation of LXX identified in step 3 as divergent from the reading(s) of LXX, and (3) any reading from the Peshiṭta, Targum, or Vulgate determined in step 4 to diverge from MT. Although the list of

readings potentially in need of retroversion is rather long, the critic will seldom find it necessary in practice to retrovert more than one or two.

Retroversion is a process requiring caution and forbearance as well as skill.[1] It is controlled by the use of a concordance to the Septuagint,[2] usually that of Hatch and Redpath.[3] This concordance provides an alphabetized list of Greek and Hebrew equivalences. Whenever it can be determined, the Hebrew word in MT corresponding to a given Greek word in LXX is listed. That is, the word that now stands in the corresponding position in MT is listed; no attempt is made to identify the Hebrew original in cases where the Greek might be thought to reflect a different reading from that of MT. The critic, therefore, will learn little from the concordance's references to the passage he is investigating; these will simply note the present correspondence between the LXX and MT readings in the passage, a correspondence of which he is already aware. The value of the concordance is rather in the information it provides about the equivalence of Greek and Hebrew words in other passages. From this the critic learns what Hebrew word or words a given Greek word corresponds to most often elsewhere This information, combined with other criteria, is often enough to permit a confident retroversion, even when the equivalence is not immediately apparent.

Consider the following examples.

2 Kings 9:7 MT והכיתה
and you will smite

LXX καὶ ἐξολεθρεύσεις
and you will utterly destroy

Does the Greek reading reflect a Hebrew reading different from that of MT? A glance at a concordance suggests that it does. *Exolethreuein* corresponds to *hikkâ* only in this passage. How, then, is the LXX reading to be retroverted? The concordance shows that *exolethreuein* corresponds to several different Hebrew verbs in other passages. The choice among them is guided by several criteria. To which of these verbs does *exolethreuein* correspond in adjacent or nearby passages? Which of them would be suitable in the present context? Would any of them be graphically similar to the reading of MT? When these criteria are applied, it becomes clear that the *Vorlage* of LXX was probably *whkrth*, "and you shall cut off." *Hikrît*

---

1. A program for responsible retroversion was set forth by M. L. Margolis in his article "Complete Induction for the Identification of the Vocabulary in the Greek Versions of the OT with its Semitic Equivalents; its Necessity and the Means of Obtaining It," *Journal of the American Oriental Society* 30 (1910):301–12. Margolis's program has now been extended by E. Tov, whose remarks offer the most useful treatment on the subject; see *The Text-Critical Use of the Septuagint in Biblical Research*, Jerusalem Biblical Studies 3 (Jerusalem: Simor, 1981), 97–179.

2. See E. Tov, "The Use of Concordances in the Reconstruction of the *Vorlage* of the LXX," *Catholic Biblical Quarterly* 40 (1978):29–36 = *Text-Critical Use of the Septuagint*, 142–54.

3. E. Hatch and H. A. Redpath, *A Concordance to the Septuagint and the Other Greek Versions of the Old Testament (Including the Apocryphal Books)*, 3 vols. (Oxford: Clarendon Press, 1892–1906; reprint, Graz: Akademische Druck- u. Verlagsanstalt, 1975).

corresponds to *exolethreuein* in nearby passages (1 Kings 18:5; 21:1; and, notably, 2 Kings 9:8), and it would fit in the present context. Moreover, *whkrth* is graphically very close to *whkyth*. Which reading, then, was original? That of MT has the better claim. *Whkrth* probably arose in the *Vorlage* of LXX in v. 7 in anticipation of *whkrth* (MT *wkrty*) in v. 8.

2 Sam. 3:14   MT   ארשׂתי   I betrothed

                   LXX   ἔλαβον   I took

The Greek word is an imprecise but acceptable equivalent of the Hebrew, and the critic might be inclined to reconstruct *'ršty* as the *Vorlage* of LXX. If he turns to the *lambanein* entry in a concordance, he will find this correspondence *(lambanein* and *'rš)* listed at 2 Sam. 3:14, but he will notice that the correspondence occurs only once elsewhere (Deut. 28:30). He will also notice, on the other hand, that forms of *lambanein* correspond to forms of *lqḥ* hundreds of times. Further investigation will show that *'rš* usually corresponds to *mnēsteuesthai*, so that the expected Greek equivalent in the present passage would be *emnēsteusamen*. Probably, then, the *Vorlage* of LXX was *lqḥty*, a reading that arose by the replacement of a distinctive or unusual word by a common one.

Retroversion is usually a straightforward process, and there is no reason to be skeptical about its validity. The Qumran discoveries brought to light numerous Hebrew readings identical to those reconstructed from the versions by critics of the past. Nevertheless, retroversion must always be undertaken with care, and it should not be attempted when sufficient evidence is lacking.

(6) Discard witnesses without independent value. When the retroverted readings are compared to the Hebrew reading(s) and to each other, it will often become apparent that one or more of the retroverted readings have no independent value. The criteria for making this determination are those discussed above. One of the retroverted Greek readings, for example, may prove to be identical to MT, and there may be reason to suspect that it was recensionally corrected toward MT. Note again that the critic will be able to make such judgments only if he is familiar with the general character of the various witnesses to his passage. He must know, in other words, which Greek witnesses tend to follow MT closely and which do not. According to the rule given above (A.1.a.1), if a Greek manuscript routinely follows MT, suggesting that it has been recensionally adjusted to MT, then its agreement with MT in a given passage cannot be considered independent evidence for the text of the passage. If, on the other hand, a Greek manuscript is generally independent of MT, then its agreement with MT in a given passage can be accepted as independent evidence, favoring the originality of the shared reading.

2. Choosing Between Readings

When the critic has evaluated the witnesses to his passage according to the criteria listed above, he may find that only one reading can be regarded as independent and authentic. If this is the case, his work is done, unless he decides to propose an emendation. Often, however, he will find that two or more readings can be so regarded. When this is the case, he must choose between the readings.

How, then, does the critic make his choice? According to what criteria does he decide that one reading is superior to another?

a. The Unreliability of External Criteria

Traditionally, textual critics have spoken of external and internal criteria for choosing between readings. External criteria are based on the merits of the manuscripts in which the readings are found, not the merits of the readings themselves. Thus the critic is advised to choose the reading found in the oldest manuscripts, or the most manuscripts, or the "best" manuscripts (i.e., those that preserve the largest number of superior readings). Such criteria, however, are unreliable. The reasoning behind them is specious, as the thoughtful critic can easily see for himself.

Consider first the criterion of the oldest manuscripts. If the biblical text had been transmitted in a few clean lines of descent, we might reasonably expect a reading in an older manuscript to be superior to a divergent one in a later manuscript. In fact, however, the *stemma* of the biblical text is extremely intricate, and its various lines of transmission are not distinct and independent. Because of recensional activity and other harmonizing tendencies, extensive contamination of one textual family by another exists. It is unsafe, therefore, to suppose that a reading in an early manuscript is superior to one in a late manuscript.

Nor is there safety in numbers. Let us suppose there are two manuscripts containing a particular reading; in one of them the reading is sound, while in the other it is corrupt. If I make a thousand copies of the second manuscript but only one of the first, will it then be correct to declare the second reading superior to the first? Of course not. The second reading will be better attested than the first by a ratio of one thousand to one, but it will still be corrupt. This is the point of the critical adage, *Manuscripta ponderantur, non numerantur,* "Manuscripts are to be weighed, not counted." The better attested reading is not necessarily preferable.

This is also true of readings found in the "best" manuscripts. It sometimes happens that one witness or another is far superior to all others in a given part of the Bible. Again and again it preserves primitive readings where other witnesses go astray. In a given case, therefore, there is a probability

71

that this same witness will have the better reading. Because we have no perfect manuscripts, however, it is *only* a probability, not a certainty. And if there is a *probability* that the reading of the good witness will be superior, then it follows that there is a *possibility* that it will be inferior. The critic, therefore, must treat the case like every other, the criterion of the best manuscripts notwithstanding.

b. Internal Criteria

The critic must base his choice between readings solely on the merits of the readings themselves, that is, on internal criteria. To a limited extent it is possible to formulate these criteria as specific guidelines to assist the critic with his task. Some of these are listed below. Most are classic critical principles, long recognized by textual scholars in all fields. They can be very useful in adding discipline and control to the critic's work. Nevertheless, as we noted in Chapter I and as the best critics have always known, the most important tools for making textual choices are good judgment and common sense. Indeed, the text-critical principles listed below are nothing more than generalizations of common sense. They serve to remind the critic of the proper course at times when his judgment fails and misdirects him.

(1) The basic principle. There is really only one principle, a fundamental maxim to which all others can be reduced. This basic principle can be expressed in more than one way, but perhaps most precisely with the question, *Utrum in alterum abiturum erat?* "Which would have changed into the other?"—that is, "Which is more likely to have given rise to the other?" This is the question the critic asks when he is ready to choose between alternative readings. When answered thoughtfully, it will provide the solution to most text-critical problems.

(2) Other rules. Like any general rule, the basic principle is so broad that it does not always give the critic enough help. Though it states the basic text-critical question clearly and establishes the proper attitude for approaching divergent readings, it does not offer specific guidelines. For this reason, other, more categorical rules have been formulated. Two of the best known are discussed below, followed by a list of several others, which will require little comment.

Note that our treatment of each of the first two rules is followed by a discussion of exceptions. The need for such discussion follows from what we have said about the final authority of good judgment and common sense in textual criticism. When the application of one of the classic principles suggests an illogical choice to the critic, he ignores the principle.

(a) *The rule of the more difficult reading.* This important and well-known guideline, which is really a restatement of the basic principle, can be expressed by the rule, *Difficilior lectio potior*, "The more difficult reading is preferable," or *Lectio difficilior praeferenda est*, "The more difficult reading is to be preferred." This rule arises from the fact that the ancient scribe, like anyone copying a manuscript, tended to see what he expected to see. That is, he tended to see the familiar. When he failed to copy what was in front of him exactly, therefore, he was much more likely to substitute the familiar for the unfamiliar than the reverse. An unusual reading, therefore, is not likely to have arisen from an ordinary one or a distinctive reading from a commonplace one. The critic favors the harder reading, the reading the scribe is less likely to have expected to see and, therefore, is less likely to have introduced erroneously into his text.

Exceptions. Sometimes a textual accident produces a bizarre or impossible reading. When this happens, the reading is usually "more difficult" than the sound reading preserved or reflected in another witness. Obviously, however, the bizarre or impossible reading is not superior. The more difficult reading is not to be preferred when it is garbage.

(b) *The rule of the shorter reading.* This principle is expressed by the rule, *Brevior lectio potior*, "The shorter reading is preferable," or *Lectio brevior praeferenda est*, "The shorter reading is to be preferred." It arises from the tendency of an ancient text to expand, especially when it was the subject of intense scribal activity. As illustrated in Chapter II.A, the text of an ancient manuscript was subject to all kinds of expansive influences—simple expansions and intrusions, dittography, glossing, conflation, and explicitation. This tendency was increased by the fact that the ancient scribes were careful to reproduce their texts fully. In their concern to preserve the text they were reluctant to omit anything. All this suggests that the shorter of two divergent readings should be given preference by the critic.

The principle of the shorter reading is illustrated by the following example.

Josh. 4:5a   MT   ויאמר להם יהושע עברו לפני ארון יהוה אלהיכם אל תוך הירדן
And Joshua said to them, "Cross over in front of the ark of Yahweh your god into the middle of the Jordan."

LXX =   ויאמר להם עברו לפני יהוה אל תוך הירדן
And he said to them, "Cross over in front of me in front of Yahweh into the middle of the Jordan."

MT has been enlarged by explicitation (*yhwš'*, "Joshua") and simple expansion (*'rwn*, "the ark of"; *'lhykm*, "your god"). Thus according to the principle of *lectio brevior*, the shorter text of LXX is generally superior. Note, however, that LXX is itself expanded by a conflation of variant readings—*lpny*, "in front of me," and *lpny yhwh*, "in front of Yahweh." Again the

73

principle of *lectio brevior* favors the shorter reading. Thus the original text of Josh. 4:5a may have read: *wy'mr lhm 'brw lpny 'l twk hyrdn,* "And he said to them, 'Cross over in front of me into the middle of the Jordan.'"

Exceptions. One of the most common textual accidents is haplography. A haplographic reading is shorter than the original from which it arose, but it is obviously not preferable to it. Thus the critic must remember that where haplography—or any accident that shortens the text (see Chapter II.B)—is suspected, the shorter reading may not be superior.

(c) *The appropriateness of a reading to its context.* This is an important positive criterion for choosing between readings. The critic gives favorable attention to a reading that suits the context. Thus, for example, a reading that conforms to an author's style is preferable to one that does not, a reading that is consistent with the viewpoint of the passage is preferable to one that is not, and so on. In applying this criterion the critic draws upon everything he knows about the context in which the reading in question occurs, including characteristics of language and thought, history, chronology, and so forth.

(d) *Readings offering stylistic improvements.* The critic is suspicious of readings that tend to conventionalize the language or style of a passage.

(e) *Modernizing readings.* Similarly, readings that tend to modernize the language or the style of a passage are suspect (cf. Chapter II.C.4).

(f) *Simplifying or trivializing readings.* Again, readings that conform the text to more familiar norms are suspect. This includes readings that simplify difficult or unusual features of grammar and syntax and readings that present common words in place of rare ones.

(g) *Readings that resolve contradictions.* When a passage somehow lacks internal consistency or logic, any reading that solves the problem must be viewed skeptically. Similarly, when a passage contradicts or otherwise clashes with another elsewhere in the Bible, a reading that resolves the tension is suspicious. At first glance this rule might seem unreasonable, but it is not. A scribe is much more likely to have introduced a harmonizing reading than one that sets up tension within his text (cf. Chapter II.D.4).

(h) *The special rule of parallel texts.* In portions of the Bible for which there are parallel texts, readings differing from those in the parallel passage are preferable to those that are the same. When working in the text of Chronicles, for example, the critic gives careful attention to any reading at variance with a reading in one of the synoptic passages in Samuel-Kings.

3. Emendation

After careful study of the various witnesses to a given reading, the critic will usually be satisfied that one or another of them preserves the original text. In such a case he will adopt its reading and move on to consideration of the next reading or some other task. Sometimes, however, he will be convinced that none of the transmitted readings is primitive. In such a case he may propose an emendation.

The term "emendation" is often misused in our field. When a critic rejects the reading of MT in favor of a reading reflected in one of the versions, we often say that he has emended the text. In fact, however, the critic has simply adopted one of the transmitted readings; he has not proposed an emendation. This is another of those infelicities that arise from our tendency to think of MT as the Hebrew text itself rather than one of the witnesses to the Hebrew text.

At least partly in consequence of this misuse of the term, we have acquired the bad habit of referring to emendation proper as "conjectural emendation." But since every emendation is conjectural, this expression is tautological. It also tends to be pejorative. Why? Not very long ago there was a period of great confidence in emendation. Critics became bold and careless, and a number of ingenious but implausible emendations found their way into scholarly books and articles, where members of the present generation still encounter them. The presence of these poor emendations in the literature has given emendation itself a bad name. Recent biblical scholarship is highly mistrustful of it.

Emendation, however, is a valuable tool that should not be discarded because of its abuse by a past generation. *Abusus non tollit usum.* With judicious application, emendation can recover portions of the biblical text that are otherwise wholly inaccessible. It should be attempted whenever the critic suspects that the primitive reading has not been preserved by any extant witness.

Because emendation is, at least in part, a matter of intuition, it is not possible to establish a set of rules that govern it. Perhaps the chief necessity is that the scholar should be self-critical in emending the text. A reading arising from emendation is subject to the same evaluative criteria as a transmitted reading. The critic must apply these to anything he proposes and pass judgment on it accordingly. Does the proposed emendation explain all the transmitted readings? Is it suited to its context? If he can answer both of these questions affirmatively, the critic need not be reticent in emending the text. If the answer to either is negative, however, he must be willing to abandon his emendation and declare the problem unsolved.

Appendix A
A Text-Critical Glossary

ALEPPO CODEX—A manuscript of MT (ca. 930 C.E.); the principal text of the edition to be published by the Hebrew University Bible Project

ANCIENT VARIANTS—Alternative attested readings, neither of which can be shown to be secondary

ANTICIPATION—A cause of copying error, occurring when a scribe's mind wanders to something that lies ahead in a familiar text

AQUILA—A second-century C.E. Greek translator, whose work is characterized by extreme literalness in translation and dogged adherence to the Hebrew text

CODEX—Sheets of papyrus or vellum folded and sewn together, the forerunner of the modern book

CODEX ALEXANDRINUS (A)—A fifth-century manuscript of LXX, complete except for portions of 1 Samuel and Psalms

CODEX LENINGRADENSIS (L)—A manuscript of MT (1008 C.E.); the principal text of *BHS*

CODEX SINAITICUS (ℵ, S)—A fourth-century manuscript of LXX

CODEX VATICANUS (B)—A fourth-century manuscript of LXX; the principal text of the Cambridge LXX, characterized by its general lack of hexaplaric revision

COLLATION—The collection and comparison of manuscripts

CONFLATION—A combination of readings from different texts or different parts of the same text

CONJECTURAL EMENDATION—Emendation

CURSIVES—Freely flowing letters often joined by ligatures, or manuscripts written with such letters (*see* MINUSCULES)

DE ROSSI VARIANTS—Readings from manuscripts and editions of MT collected by J. B. de Rossi (1784–88)

DEFECTIVE SPELLING—The older Hebrew orthography, making limited use of *matres lectionis*

DITTOGRAPHY—A copying error, occurring when a scribe copied a letter or several letters twice

EARLY VARIANTS—Ancient variants

ECLECTIC TRANSLATION—An attempt to render an original text by critically selecting readings from various witnesses

EMENDATION—An attempt to reconstruct an original reading that has not survived among extant witnesses

EPEXEGETICAL PLUS—An insertion of explanatory matter into a text by a scribe

EXPANSION—Any increase in the length of a text

GLOSS—A scribal insertion intended to explain an obscure word or phrase

GRAPHIC CONFUSION—A copying error occurring when a letter is mistaken for another with a similar form

HAPLOGRAPHY—A copying error involving a loss of text when two identical or similar letters or groups of letters occur in sequence and are copied only once; by extension, parablepsis caused by repeated sequences of letters *(homoioarkton* or *homoioteleuton)*

HARMONIZATION—The elimination of contradictions within a text by a scribal insertion or alteration

HEXAPLA—Origen's six-column Bible (230–45 C.E.), containing in columns (1) the Hebrew text, (2) a Greek transliteration of the Hebrew text, (3) the translation of Aquila, (4) the translation of Symmachus, (5) the LXX, with annotations and adjustments toward the Hebrew text, and (6) the translation or revision of Theodotion

HEXAPLARIC REVISION—Adjustment of Greek Bible manuscripts made on the basis of readings from the fifth column of the Hexapla and thus tending to conform the LXX to the Hebrew of Origen's time

HIATUS—A gap in a manuscript

HOMOIOARKTON—A cause of copying error involving a loss of text when identical or similar sequences of letters at the beginning of two words or phrases are read as one

HOMOIOTELEUTON—A cause of copying error involving a loss of text when identical or similar sequences of letters at the end of two words or phrases are read as one

JEROME—A fourth-century C.E. scholar who revised and retranslated the Latin Bible

Kaige RECENSION—A revision of the Old Greek toward an early forerunner of MT in the early first century C.E., characterized by (among other things) the translation of Hebrew *wĕgam*, "and also," by Greek *kai ge*

KENNICOTT VARIANTS—Readings from manuscripts and editions of MT published by B. Kennicott (1776–80)

Kĕtîb—The "written" form of a word in the Hebrew Bible, especially as distinct from the *qĕrê*

Lapsus calami—A slip of the pen, a scribal error

LUCIAN—A fourth-century C.E. Christian martyr, traditionally responsible for a revision of the Greek Bible characterized by a full text and classic (Attic) forms

MAJUSCULES—Greek manuscripts written in capital letters, used until the tenth century C.E.

MASSORA—A corpus of notes on the text and transmission of the Hebrew Bible

MASSORETIC TEXT (MT)—The traditional rabbinic text of the Hebrew Bible, deriving from certain Tiberian families of the sixth to tenth centuries C.E. and characterized by vocalization and Massora

Matres lectionis—"Mothers of the reading," letters used to mark vowels in a Hebrew text

METATHESIS—Transposition

MINUS—A portion of text that is missing in comparison to another text

77

MINUSCULES—Greek manuscripts written in small letters, used from the ninth century C.E. onward

OLD GREEK—The original Greek translation of the Hebrew Bible, forerunner of the LXX

OLD LATIN—The earliest Latin translations of the Greek Bible, surviving only in fragments

ORTHOGRAPHY—The rules and conventions of spelling

PALEOGRAPHY—The study of ancient scripts, especially their form and development

PARABLEPSIS—A scribal oversight, sometimes caused by *homoioarkton* or *homoioteleuton*

PESHIṬṬA—The standard form of the Syriac Bible

Plene SPELLING—The later, "full" Hebrew orthography, making more use of *matres lectionis*

PLUS—A portion of a text not found in another text

PRIMITIVE—Not secondary or derivative

PROTO-LUCIANIC—Pertaining to materials sharing the character of Lucian's text but antedating his work, which are taken as evidence for a recension of the Old Greek toward a Hebrew text current in Palestine at the turn of the era or earlier

PROTO-THEODOTIONIC—Pertaining to materials sharing the character of Theodotion's text but antedating his work, which are taken as evidence for a recension of the Old Greek text toward an early forerunner of MT in the first century C.E. (cf. *Kaige* RECENSION)

Qěrê—The "read" or vocalized form of a word in the Hebrew Bible, especially as distinct from the *kětîb*

READING—Any discrete group of letters or words

RECENSION—Revision of a manuscript to bring it into conformity with another manuscript

REMINISCENCE—A cause of copying error, occurring when a scribe's mind wanders back to something he copied previously

RETROVERSION—The retranslation of a translated text back into the original language

SAMARITAN PENTATEUCH—The first five books of the Bible in the form transmitted within the Samaritan community

SCROLL—A rolled document written on leather or papyrus

SECONDARY—Derived from another reading

SEPTUAGINT (LXX)—Strictly, the oldest Greek version of the Pentateuch, but by extension the Greek Bible as a whole in its earliest form (the Old Greek); by further extension, the Greek Bible in all its variety, early and late

SIMPLE EXPANSION—The spontaneous and erroneous insertion of material into a text, especially as distinct from epexegetical expansion or expansion caused by mechanical accidents

SYMMACHUS—A second-century C.E. translator, whose work is characterized by good Greek style and close adherence to the Hebrew text

TARGUM—One of the Aramaic translations of the Hebrew Bible

THEODOTION—A second-century C.E. Greek translator or reviser, whose work is characterized by close adherence to the Hebrew text and extensive use of transliteration (*see also* PROTO-THEODOTIONIC)

Tiqqûnê sôpĕrîm—"The errors of the scribes"

TRANSPOSITION—A copying error involving an exchange in the position of two or (rarely) more letters within a word

UNCIALS—Majuscules

VARIANT—An attested reading that differs from another attested reading; loosely, an attested reading that differs from the reading of MT

VERSION—A translation, especially of the Hebrew Bible

Vorlage—The text from which a translation was made

VULGATE—Jerome's Latin translation

WITNESS—Any manuscript (including a translation of a manuscript, a fragment of a manuscript, or a quotation from a manuscript) providing testimony to a text

Appendix B
Bibliography of Primary Sources†

A. CRITICAL EDITIONS
1. The Massoretic Text

Elliger, K., and W. Rudolph, eds. *Biblia Hebraica Stuttgartensia.* Stuttgart: Deutsche Bibelstiftung, 1967–77.

Now the standard scholarly edition of MT, this is the completely revised successor to the third edition of Kittel's *Biblia Hebraica*. Its textual basis is the Codex Leningradensis.

Goshen-Gottstein, M. H., ed. *The Book of Isaiah. Sample Edition with Introduction* (1965); *Volume One: Chapters 1–22* (1975); *Volume Two: Chapters 22–44* (1981). Jerusalem: Magnes Press.

These are the first fascicles of the Hebrew University Bible Project's ambitious new edition of MT. The textual basis is the Aleppo Codex.

2. The Samaritan Pentateuch

von Gall, A., ed. *Der hebräischer Pentateuch der Samaritaner.* 5 vols. Berlin: de Gruyter, 1914–18; reprint, 1966.

3. The Septuagint

Two modern critical editions are available, neither complete. The decision to use the Cambridge LXX or the Göttingen LXX is usually dictated by the book in which the critic is working. If the text under examination is that of Genesis, Numbers, Deuteronomy, or Esther, however, there is a choice. In this case the recent (and therefore up-to-date) Göttingen volumes are preferable.

Brooke, A. E., N. McLean, and H. St. J. Thackeray, eds. *The Old Testament in Greek According to the Text of the Codex Vaticanus.* 3 vols. Cambridge: Cambridge University Press, 1906– .

This is the Cambridge LXX. The published volumes include the texts of the books of Genesis through Tobit in the LXX order. (Nothing has appeared since 1940!) The textual basis is the Codex Vaticanus or, when it fails, the best extant text.

† The abbreviations are in conformity with those of the *Journal of Biblical Literature.* See also J. A. Fitzmyer, *The Dead Sea Scrolls: Major Publications and Tools for Study* (Missoula, Mont.: Scholars Press, 1977).

Ziegler, J., et al., eds. *Septuaginta. Vetus Testamentum Graecum auctoritate Academiae Scientarium Gottingensis editum.* Göttingen: Vandenhoeck & Ruprecht, 1931– .
This is the Göttingen LXX. Published volumes include the texts of the books of Genesis, Numbers, Deuteronomy, Esther, Job, the Twelve Prophets, Isaiah, Jeremiah, Lamentations, Ezekiel, and Daniel, as well as certain apocryphal books. The text is "critical," that is, eclectic.

Rahlfs, A., ed. *Septuaginta, id est Vetus Testamentum Graece iuxta LXX interpretes.* 2 vols. Stuttgart: Privileg. Württ. Bibelanstalt, 1935.
Rahlfs's edition is complete and useful for quick reference, but the apparatus is too small for most text-critical needs. For projects involving the texts of books not yet published by the Cambridge or Göttingen LXX (i.e., Psalms, Proverbs, Ecclesiastes, or Song of Solomon), the critic should consult one of the two out-of-date but complete editions cited below.

Holmes, R., and J. Parsons, eds. *Vetus Testamentum Graecum variis lectionibus.* 5 vols. Oxford: Clarendon Press, 1798–1827.

Swete, H. B., ed. *The Old Testament in Greek According to the Septuagint.* 3 vols. Cambridge: Cambridge University Press, 1887–94.

4. The Peshiṭta (Syriac)

Peshiṭta Institute, ed. *The Old Testament in Syriac According to the Peshiṭta Version.* Leiden: E. J. Brill, 1972– .
Volumes published to date include the texts of the following books: Genesis, Exodus, Judges, 1 and 2 Samuel, 1 and 2 Kings, the Twelve Prophets, Psalms, Job, Proverbs, Qoheleth, Song of Songs, and certain apocryphal books.

5. The Targums

Sperber, A., ed. *The Bible in Aramaic. . . .* 4 vols. Leiden: E. J. Brill, 1959–73.
Sperber's edition does not include the Palestinian Targum (Yerushalmi) to the Pentateuch, now known in almost complete form in the Codex Neofiti I (Ni 1). Its *editio princeps* is:

Díez Macho, A., ed. *Neophyti I, Targum Palastinense Ms de la Biblioteca Vaticana.* 6 vols. Madrid: Consejo Superior de Investigaciones Científicas, 1968– .

6. The Old Latin

Fischer, B., et al., eds. *Vetus Latina. Die Reste der altlateinischen Bibel.* Freiburg: Herder, 1949– .
This is the edition of the Beuron Institute, successor to P. Sabatier's *Bibliorum sacrorum latinae versiones antiquae seu Vetus Itala* (Rheims, 1745–49). Volume 1 contains a list of manuscripts and sigla, but of the actual texts only Genesis among the Old Testament books has appeared so far. For the time being, therefore, the critic must rely on the citations of the OL found in the critical editions of the LXX.

7. The Vulgate

Gasquet, A., ed. *Biblia sacra . . . ad codicum fidem.* Rome: typis polyglottis Vaticanis, 1926– .

Complete through Baruch. The useful *editio minor* is:

Weber, R., ed. *Biblia sacra iuxta Vulgatam versionem*. Rev. ed. Stuttgart: Württembergische Bibelanstalt, 1975.

B. MANUSCRIPTS FROM THE JUDEAN DESERT

1. Qumran

Qumran Cave 1

1QGen	Barthélemy, D., and J. T. Milik. *Discoveries in the Judaean Desert of Jordan. I. Qumrân Cave 1*. Oxford: Clarendon Press, 1955. = *DJD* I 49–50.
1QExod	*DJD* I 50–51.
1QLev	*DJD* I 51–54.
1QDeut^a,b	*DJD* I 54–62.
1QJudg	*DJD* I 62–64.
1QSam	*DJD* I 64–65.
1QIsa^a	Burrows, M., ed. *The Dead Sea Scrolls of St. Mark's Monastery* 1. New Haven, Conn.: American Schools of Oriental Research, 1950.
1QIsa^b	Sukenik, E. L. *The Dead Sea Scrolls of the Hebrew University*. Jerusalem: Magnes Press, 1955. Additional fragments in *DJD* I 66–68.
1QEzek	*DJD* I 68–69.
1QPs^a–c	*DJD* I 69–72.
1QDan^a,b	Trever, J. "Completion of the Publication of Some Fragments from Qumran Cave I." *RevQ* 5/19 (1965):323–44; also *DJD* I 150–52.

Qumran Cave 2

2QGen	Baillet, M., J. T. Milik, and R. de Vaux. *Discoveries in the Judaean Desert of Jordan. III. Les "petites grottes" de Qumrân*. Oxford: Clarendon Press, 1962. = *DJD* III 48–49.
2QExod^a–c	*DJD* III 49–56.
2QpaleoLev	*DJD* III 56–57.
2QNum^a–d	*DJD* III 57–60.
2QDeut^a–c	*DJD* III 60–62.
2QJer	*DJD* III 62–69.
2QPs	*DJD* III 69–71.
2QJob	*DJD* III 71.
2QRuth^a,b	*DJD* III 71–74.

Qumran Cave 3

3QEzek	*DJD* III 94.
3QPs2	*DJD* III 94.
3QLam	*DJD* III 95.

Qumran Cave 4

4QExod^a	Cross, F. M. *The Ancient Library of Qumran.* Rev. Ed., 184–85, n. 31.° Garden City, N.Y.: Doubleday & Co., Anchor Books A 272, 1961.
4QExod^c	Cross, F. M. "The Song of the Sea and Canaanite Myth." *JTC* 5 (1968):1–25 [13–16].°
4QExod^f	Cross, F. M. In *Scrolls from the Wilderness of the Dead Sea.* Smithsonian Institution Exhibit Catalogue. ASOR: Cambridge, Mass., 1965. = *SWDS* 14, 23.°
4QpaleoExod^m	Skehan, P. W. "Exodus in the Samaritan Recension from Qumran." *JBL* 74 (1955):182–87.°
4QLXXNum	Skehan, P. W. "The Qumran Manuscripts and Textual Criticism." *Volume du Congrès, Strasbourg 1956,* 148–60 [155–56].° VTSup 4; Leiden: E. J. Brill, 1957.
4QLXXLev^a	Skehan. "Qumran Manuscripts" [157–60].°
4QDeutⁿ	Cross, F. M. In *SWDS* 20, 31–32. Cf. Stegemann, H. ". . . Hinweis auf eine unedierte Handschrift aus Höhle 4Q mit Exzerpten aus dem Deuteronomium." *RevQ* 6/22 (1967):193–227 [217–27].°
4QDeut^q	Skehan, P. W. "A Fragment of the 'Song of Moses' (Deut. 32) from Qumran." *BASOR* 136 (1954):12–15.°
4QSam^a	Cross, F. M. "A New Qumran Biblical Fragment Related to the Original Hebrew Underlying the Septuagint." *BASOR* 132 (1953):15–26.°
4QSam^b	Cross, F. M. "The Oldest Manuscripts from Qumran." *JBL* 74 (1955):147–72 [165–72].°
4QSam^c	Ulrich, E. C. "4QSam^c: A Fragmentary Manuscript of 2 Samuel 14–15 from the Scribe of the *Serek Hay-yaḥad* (1QS)." *BASOR* 235 (1979):1–25.
4QIsa^a	Muilenburg, J. "Fragments of Another Qumran Isaiah Scroll." *BASOR* 135 (1954):28–32.
4QJer^{a,b}	Janzen, J. G. *Studies in the Text of Jeremiah,* 173–84 [4QJer^a: 174–81; 4QJer^b: 181–84].° HSM 6. Cambridge, Mass.: Harvard University Press, 1973.
4QXII^c	Testuz, M. "Deux fragments inédits des manuscrits de la Mer Morte." *Sem* 5 (1955):38–39.°
4QXII^d	Wolff, H. W. *Hosea: A Commentary on the Book of the Prophet Hosea.* Translated by G. Stansell. v. Hermeneia. Philadelphia: Fortress Press, 1974. Cf. G.-W. Nebe, "Eine neue Hosea-Handschrift aus Höhle 4 von Qumran," *ZAW* 91 (1979): 292–94; L. A. Sinclair, "A Qumran Biblical Fragment: Hosea 4QXII^d (Hosea 1:7–2:5)," *BASOR* 239 (1980):61–65.°

° Partial or preliminary publication only

4QPs[b]	Skehan, P. W. "A Psalm Manuscript from Qumran (4QPs[b])." *CBQ* 26 (1964):313–22.°
4QPs[f]	Starcky, J. "Psaumes apocryphes de la grotte 4 de Qumrân (4QPs[f] VII–X)." *RB* 73 (1966):353–71.
4QPs[q]	Milik, J. T. "Deux documents inédits du Désert de Juda." *Biblica* 38 (1957):245–68 [245–55].
4QPs89	Milik, J. T. "Fragment d'une source de psautier (4QPs89). . . ." *RB* 73 (1966):94–106 [94–104].
4QQoh[a]	Muilenburg, J. "A Qoheleth Scroll from Qumran." *BASOR* 135 (1954):20–28.

Qumran Cave 5

5QDeut	*DJD* III 169–71.
5QKgs	*DJD* III 171–72.
5QIsa	*DJD* III 173.
5QAmos	*DJD* III 173–74.
5QPs	*DJD* III 174.
5QLam[a,b]	*DJD* III 174–78.

Qumran Cave 6

6QpaleoGen	*DJD* III 105–6.
6QpaleoLev	*DJD* III 106.
6QDeut	*DJD* III 106–7.
6QKgs	*DJD* III 107–12.
6QPs	*DJD* III 112.
6QCant	*DJD* III 112–14.
6QDan	*DJD* III 114–16.

Qumran Cave 7

7QExod gr	*DJD* III 142–43.

Qumran Cave 8

8QGen	*DJD* III 147–48.
8QPs	*DJD* III 148–49.

Qumran Cave 11

11QLev	van der Ploeg, J. P. M. "Lèv. IX, 23—X, 2 dans un texte de Qumran." In *Bibel und Qumran.* Edited by S. Wagner, 153–55. H. Bardtke FS. Berlin: Evangelische Haupt-Bibelgesellschaft, 1968.
11QpaleoLev	Freedman, D. N., and K. A. Mathews. *The Paleo-Hebrew Leviticus Scroll.* ASOR: Winona Lake, Ind.: Eisenbrauns, 1985.

° Partial or preliminary publication only

11QEzek	Brownlee, W. H. "The Scroll of Ezekiel from the Eleventh Qumran Cave." *RevQ* 4/13 (1963):11–28.
11QPs^a	Sanders, J. A. *Discoveries in the Judaean Desert of Jordan. IV. The Psalms Scroll of Qumrân Cave 11 (11QPsª).* Oxford: Clarendon Press, 1965.
	Sanders, J. A. *The Dead Sea Psalms Scroll.* Ithaca, N.Y.: Cornell University Press, 1967.
11QPs^b	van der Ploeg, J. P. M. "Fragments d'un manuscrit de psaumes de Qumran (11QPsᵇ)." *RB* 74 (1967):408–12.
11QPs^c	van der Ploeg, J. P. M. "Fragments d'un psautier de Qumrân." *Symbolae biblicae et mesopotamicae Francisco Mario Theodoro de Liagre Böhl dedicatae.* Edited by M. A. Beek et al., 208–9. Leiden: E. J. Brill, 1973.
11QPsAp^a	van der Ploeg, J. P. M. "Le psaume xci dans une recension de Qumran." *RB* 72 (1965):210–17.

2. Masada

MasGen	Yadin, Y. "The Excavation of Masada—1963/64: Preliminary Report." *IEJ* 15 (1965):1–20 [104–5].
	Yadin, Y. *Masada: Herod's Fortress and the Zealots' Last Stand,* 179. ° New York: Random House, 1966.
MasLev	Yadin, Y. "Excavation of Masada" [104]; *Masada,* 172, 179. °
MasDeut	Yadin, Y. *Masada,* 187–89. °
MasEzek	Yadin, Y. *Masada,* 187–89. °
MasPs	Yadin, Y. "Excavation of Masada" [103–4]; *Masada,* 170–72. °

3. Wadi Murabba'at

MurGen	Beniot, P., J. T. Milik, and R. de Vaux. *Discoveries in the Judaean Desert of Jordan. II. Les grottes de Murabba'at.* Oxford: Clarendon Press, 1961. = *DJD* II 75–77.
MurGen^(b)	Puech, E. "Fragment d'un rouleau de la Genèse provenant du Désert de Juda (Gen. 33, 18—34, 3)." *RevQ* 10/38 (1980):163–66. °
MurExod	*DJD* II 77–78.
MurNum	*DJD* II 78.
MurDeut	*DJD* II 78–79.
MurIsa	*DJD* II 79–80.
MurXII	*DJD* II 181–205.

4. Naḥal Ḥever (Wadi Habra)

?ḤevGen	Burchard, C. "Gen 35 6–10 und 36 5–12 MT aus der Wüste Juda (Naḥal Ḥever, Cave of the Letters?)." *ZAW* 78 (1966):71–75. Cf. *ADAJ* 2 (1953):pl. xii. °

° Partial or preliminary publication only

5/6HevNum	Yadin, Y. "Expedition D—The Cave of the Letters." *IEJ* 12 (1962):227–57 [229].°
5/6HevPs	Yadin, Y. "Expedition D." *IEJ* 11 (1961):36–52 [40].
8HevXII gr	Barthélemy, D. *Les Devanciers d'Aquila,* 163–78. VTSup 10. Leiden: E. J. Brill, 1963.

° Partial or preliminary publication only

Appendix C
Textual Characteristics of the
Books of the Hebrew Bible†

As stressed in the preceding chapters, the critic must be familiar with the general characteristics of the major witnesses to a portion of text under investigation. The purpose of the following tabulation, therefore, is to provide an initial orientation to the most important witnesses to the text of each book of the Hebrew Bible. Note, however, that such an orientation is only a starting point. A thorough acquaintance with any group of witnesses comes only from extensive experience of the text—that is, from long hours of work with the manuscripts; it cannot be acquired in abstraction from the readings themselves. After the critic has begun work, therefore, he will want to revise the descriptions offered here as the evidence dictates.

The tabulation is arranged as follows:

MT: a comment on the condition of the text in the book in question

LXX: A description of the major manuscripts, including comments on the character of the translation they contain (literal, free, etc.), their relationships to MT and each other, and their value as witnesses to the Old Greek text (OG)

Other Witnesses: Comments where appropriate

Scrolls: Reference to biblical manuscripts from Qumran (Q) or other sites (Hev = Naḥal Ḥever, Mas = Masada, Mur = Wadi Murabba'at). [NOTE: Only biblical manuscripts (excluding phylacteries and mezuzas) are listed; for phylacteries and mezuzas, as well as pesher and targum materials (which frequently offer valuable textual evidence), see J. A. Fitzmyer, *The Dead Sea Scrolls: Major Publications and Tools for Study*, Sources for Biblical Study 8 (Missoula, Mont.: Scholars Press, 1975; suppl. 1977), and the regularly published bibliographies in *RevQ*.]

Papyri: Reference to papyri of the Greek Bible of special textual importance. [NOTE: Most often, these are cited in modern critical editions of LXX.]

Parallels: Citation of synoptic passages

† The abbreviations are in conformity with those of the *Journal of Biblical Literature*. See also J. A. Fitzmyer, *The Dead Sea Scrolls: Major Publications and Tools for Study* (Missoula, Mont.: Scholars Press, 1977).

Pentateuch
MT: Excellent condition, generally free from expansions and serious problems
LXX: Literal translation, idiomatic Greek (B); limited variety among manuscripts;
B normally the best witness to the OG
Samaritan: Generally expansionistic, with some sectarian readings and insertion of
parallel passages into the text

Genesis (see also Pentateuch)
LXX: B is lacking through 46:28a; Cambridge LXX uses A
Scrolls: 1QGen (1:18–21; 3:11–14; 22:13–15; 23:17–19; 24:22–24); 2QGen (19:27–
28; 36:6, 35–37); 6QpaleoGen (6:13–21); 8QGen (17:12–19); MasGen (46:7–11°);
MurGen (32:4–5, 30; 32:33—33:1; 34:5–7; 34:30—35:1, 4–7); MurGen(b) (33:18—
34:3); ?HevGen (35:6–10; 36:5–12)
Papyri: Berlin Genesis = Göttingen 911 (chaps. 1—35), a prehexaplaric manuscript
with affinities for the hexaplaric text and the following two papyri; Chester Beatty
P. 961 (parts of chaps. 9—15; 17—44) and P. 962 (parts of chaps. 8—9; 24—25;
30—35; 39—46), valuable as witnesses to OG, especially in view of the failure of B
Parallels: Extensive parallels and partial parallels in Chronicles

Exodus (see also Pentateuch)
LXX: Substantial differences from MT in chaps. 35—40
Scrolls: 1QExod (16:12–16; 19:24—20:1; 20:5–6; 20:25—21:1, 4–5); 2QExoda
(1:11–14; 7:1–4; 9:27–29; 11:3–7; 12:32–41; 21:18–20[?]; 26:11–13; 30:21[?], 23–25;
32:32–34); 2QExodb (4:31; 12:26–27[?]; 18:21–22; 19:9; 21:37—22:2, 15–19;
27:17–19; 31:16–17; 34:10); 2QExodc (5:3–5); 4QExoda (1:1–5°); 4QExodc
(15:16–18°); 4QExodf (40:8–27°); 4QpaleoExodm (6:25—7:19°); 7QExod gr
(28:4–7 [papyrus]); MurExod (4:27–31; 5:3; 6:5–11)
Parallels: Partial parallels in Chronicles

Leviticus (see also Pentateuch)
Scrolls: 1QLev (11:10–11; 19:30–34; 20:20–24; 21:24—22:6; 23:4–8); 2QpaleoLev
(11:22–29); 4QLXXLeva (26:2–16°); 6QpaleoLev (8:12–13); 11QLev (9:23—
10:2); 11QpaleoLev (parts of 4:24—27:19); MasLev (4:3–9°)

Numbers (see also Pentateuch)
Scrolls: 1QLev [sic] (1:48–50; 36:7–8[?]); 2QNuma (3:38–41; 3:51—4:3); 2QNumb
(33:47–53); 2QNumc (7:88); 2QNumd (18:8–9); 4QLXXNum (3:38—4:14°); 5/6
HevNum (20:7–8°); MurNum (34:10; 36:7–11)
Papyri: Chester Beatty P. 963 (parts of chaps. 5—8 and 21—35), an important pre-
hexaplaric witness to OG
Parallels: Parallels and partial parallels in Chronicles

° Partial or preliminary publication only

Deuteronomy (*see also* Pentateuch)
LXX: Some hexaplaric readings in B, which may be a less reliable witness to OG than elsewhere in the Pentateuch
Scrolls: 1QDeut^a (1:22–25; 4:47–49; 8:18–19; 9:27–28; 11:27–30; 13:1–6, 13–14; 14:21, 24–25; 16:4, 6–7); 1QDeut^b (1:9–13; 8:8–9; 9:10; 11:30–31; 15:14–15; 17:16; 21:8–9; 24:10–16; 25:13–18; 28:44–48; 29:9–20; 30:19—31:10, 12–13; 32:17–29; 33:12–19, 21–24); 2QDeut^a (1:7–9); 2QDeut^b (17:12–15); 2QDeut^c (10:8–12); 4QDeut^n (5:1—6:1; 8:5–10°); 4QDeut^q (32:37–43°); 5QDeut (7:15–24; 8:5—9:2); 6QDeut (26:19[?]); MurDeut (10:1–3; 11:2–3; 12:25–26; 14:29—15:1)
Papyri: Rylands P. Greek 458 = Göttingen 967 (23:24—24:3; 25:1–3; 26:12, 17–19; 28:31–33); manuscript 89 of P. Fouad 266 (17:14—33:29); Chester Beatty P. 963 (parts of chaps. 1—7; 11—12; 28—34); all pre-hexaplaric witnesses to the OG, especially important in view of the problems in B

Joshua
MT: Expansionistic
LXX: Literal translation, non-idiomatic Greek (B); limited variety among manuscripts except in city and boundary lists, where B and A diverge; B (OG) substantially shorter than MT; Lucianic witnesses include the minuscules gnw tpd and b (1:1—2:18a only) and perhaps the uncial K (Cambridge LXX)
Parallels: Parallels and partial parallels in Chronicles

Judges
MT: Exceptionally good (not in the Song of Deborah), approaching the Pentateuch in quality
LXX: Literal translation, non-idiomatic (A) or wooden (B) Greek; uniquely wide divergence between A and B; hexaplaric revision in A, *kaige* revision in B; Lucianic witnesses, including the minuscules gnw tpd and possibly the uncial K (Cambridge LXX), especially important for OG in view of the character of B
OL: Lucianic, especially important for OG because of the *kaige* character of LXX^B
Scrolls: 1QJudg (6:20–22; 8:1[?]; 9:1–6, 28–31, 40–43, 48–49)

1 and 2 Samuel
MT: Defective, especially troubled by haplography; expansions in the Goliath pericope
LXX: Literal translation, non-idiomatic or (in *kaige* sections) wooden Greek (B); *kaige* revision in B in 2 Sam. 10:1—24:25; Lucianic witnesses, including the minuscules boc$_2$e$_2$ (Cambridge LXX), especially important for reconstructing the OG where B is *kaige*
OL: Lucianic, especially important for reconstructing OG in the *kaige* section of LXX^B

° Partial or preliminary publication only

Scrolls: 1QSam (2 Sam. 20:6–10; 21:16–18; 23:9–12); 4QSam^a (1 Sam. 1:22—2:6; 2:16–25°); 4QSam^b (1 Sam. 16:1–11; 19:10–17; 21:3–10; 23:9–17°); 4QSam^c (1 Sam. 25:30–32; 2 Sam. 14:7—15:15)
Parallels: Extensive parallels in Chronicles; Psalm 18 = 2 Samuel 22

1 and 2 Kings
MT: Generally sound, but with expansive tendency
LXX: Shorter than MT, but with notable pluses, rearrangements, and other differences; literal translation, non-idiomatic or (in *kaige* sections) wooden Greek (B); *kaige* revision in B in 1 Kings 1:1—2:11, in 1 Kings 22, and in all of 2 Kings; Lucianic witnesses, including the minuscules borc$_2$e$_2$ (Cambridge LXX), especially important for reconstructing OG in sections where B is *kaige*
OL: Lucianic, important for reconstructing OG, especially where LXX^B is *kaige*
Scrolls: 5QKgs (1 Kings 1:1, 16–17, 27–37); 6QKgs (1 Kings 3:12–14; 12:28–31; 22:28–31; 2 Kings 5:26; 6:32; 7:8–10; 7:20—8:5; 9:1–2; 10:19–21)
Parallels: Isaiah 36:1—38:8+39:1–8 = 2 Kings 18:13—20:19; Jeremiah 52 = 2 Kings 24:18—25:30; extensive parallels in Chronicles

Isaiah
MT: Expansionistic
LXX: Very free translation, verging on paraphrase, except in chaps. 36—39, where it is relatively literal; B expansionistic with insertions from parallel passages and hexaplaric revision, not OG; Lucianic witnesses, including 22, 36, 48, 51, 62, 93, and 147 (Göttingen LXX), very important for reconstructing OG in view of the condition and character of B
Scrolls: 1QIsa^a (complete except for small lacunae); 1QIsa^b (parts of 7:22—66:24); 4QIsa^a (12:5—13:16; 22:13—23:6); 5QIsa (40:16, 18–19); MurIsa (1:4–14)
Papyri: Chester Beatty P. 965, fragmentary (parts of chaps. 8—19; 38—45; 54—60) but important for reconstructing OG in view of the condition of B
Parallels: 2 Kings 18:13—20:19 = Isa. 36:1—38:8+39:1–8; Micah 4:1–4 = Isa. 2:2–5

Jeremiah
MT: Expansionistic
LXX: Literal translation, non-idiomatic Greek (B); B may be OG only in chaps. 1—28; chaps. 29—52 a different translation or revision; about 1/7 shorter than MT, different order of materials; Lucianic witnesses include 22, 36, 48, 51, 62, 93, and 147 (Göttingen LXX)
Scrolls: 2QJer (42:14; 43:8–11; 44:1–3, 12–14; 46:27—47:7; 48:7, 25–39, 43–45; 49:10); 4QJer^a (7:29—9:2; 9:7–14; 10:9–14; 11:3–6; 12:3–6; 12:17—13:7; 14:4–7; 15:1–2; 17:8–26; 18:15—19:1; 22:4–16°); 4QJer^b (9:22—10:18; 43:3–9; 50:4–6°)
Papyri: Chester Beatty P. 966 (parts of chaps. 4—14)
Parallels: 2 Kings 24:18—25:30 = Jeremiah 52

° Partial or preliminary publication only

Ezekiel
MT: Expansionistic, some sections especially troubled
LXX: Literal translation, non-idiomatic Greek (B); B may be OG only in chaps.
1—27+40—48; chaps. 28—39 a different translation or revision; Lucianic witnesses, including 22, 36, 48, 51, 62, 93, and 147 (Göttingen LXX), important for
the reconstruction of OG, especially in chaps. 28—39
OL: Lucianic, important for the reconstruction of OG, especially in chaps. 28—39,
where LXX^B is not OG
Scrolls: 1QEzek (4:16—5:1); 3QEzek (16:30–31); 11QEzek (4:3–6; 5:11–17; 7:9–12;
10:11; 13:17)
Papyri: Chester Beatty–John H. Scheide P. 967 and P. 968 (parts of chaps. 11—17;
19—39), important pre-hexaplaric witness to OG

Minor Prophets
MT: Expansionistic
LXX: Literal translation, non-idiomatic Greek (B); close to MT in character;
Lucianic witnesses include 22, 36, 48, 51, and often 62 and 147
Scrolls: 8HevXII gr (Jonah 1:14--Zech. 9:4); MurXII (Joel 2:20—Zech. 1:4); see
also "Hosea"
Papyri: Freer Greek MS (Amos–Malachi), affinities with Lucianic manuscripts

Hosea (see also Minor Prophets)
MT: Very corrupt, many unintelligible passages
Scrolls: 4QXII^c (13:15—14:1, 3–6°); 4QXII^d (1:7–2:5°)

Joel (see also Minor Prophets)
MT: Well preserved
LXX: Four chapters to MT's three (MT 2:1–27 = LXX 2; MT 2:28–32 = LXX 3; MT
3 = LXX 4)

Amos (see also Minor Prophets)
MT: Well preserved
Scrolls: 5QAmos (1:3–5)

Obadiah (see also Minor Prophets)
MT: Well preserved

Jonah (see also Minor Prophets)
MT: Very well preserved

Micah (see also Minor Prophets)
MT: Generally poor condition
Parallels: Isa. 2:2–5 = Micah 4:1–4

° Partial or preliminary publication only

Nahum (*see* Minor Prophets)

Habakkuk (*see also* Minor Prophets)
LXX: Special problem of the divergence between B and the so-called Barberini text in chap. 3

Zephaniah (*see* Minor Prophets)

Haggai (*see* Minor Prophets)

Zechariah (*see* Minor Prophets)

Malachi (*see* Minor Prophets)

Hagiographa
MT: Generally expansionistic

Psalms
MT: Fair condition
LXX: Literal, non-idiomatic Greek (B); limited range of variants; significant differences in arrangement from MT; B lacks Pss. 105:27—137:6; Lucianic witnesses include 108, 144, 147, 185 (Gottingen, LXX)
Scrolls: 1QPs^a (86:5–8; 92:12–14; 94:16; 95:11—96:2; 119:31–34, 43–48, 77–79); 1QPs^b (126:6; 127:1–5); 1QPs^c (44:3–5, 7, 9, 23–25); 2QPs (103:2–11; 104:6–11); 3QPs2 (2:6–7); 4QPs^b (parts of Pss. 91; 92; 94; 99; 100; 102; 103; 112; 116; and 118*); 4QPs^f (109:23–31); 4QPs^q (31:24–25; 33:1–18; 35:4–20); 4QPs89 (89:20–23, 26–28, 31); 5QPs (119:99–101, 104, 113–20, 138–42); 6QPs (78:26–37); 8QPs (17:5–9; 18:6–9, 10–13); 11QPs^a (parts of Pss. 101—145 with noncanonical psalms); 11QPs^b (parts of Pss. 141; 133; 144; 118); 11QPs^c (17:9–15; 18:1–12); 11QPsAp^a (noncanonical psalms with parts of Psalm 91); 5/6HevPs (15:1–15; 16:1*); MasPs (81:3—85:10; 150:1–6*)
Parallels: Psalm 14 = Psalm 53; Ps. 40:14–18 = Psalm 70; Pss. 57:8–12+60:7–14 = Psalm 108; 2 Samuel 22 = Psalm 18; 1 Chron. 16:8–36 = Pss. 105:1–15+96:1–13+106:1, 47–48

Job
MT: Expansionistic
LXX: OG 1/6 shorter than MT, supplemented in B by *kaige* additions; translation very free (OG) to very literal (*kaige*), idiomatic Greek
Scrolls: 2QJob (33:28–30)

Proverbs
MT: Expansionistic

* Partial or preliminary publication only

LXX: Free paraphrase, midrashic tendencies; significant differences in arrangement

Ruth
MT: Expansionistic
LXX: Literal translation (B); *kaige* revision in B
Scrolls: 2QRuth[a] (2:13—3:8; 4:3–4); 2QRuth[b] (3:13–18)
Parallels: 1 Chron. 2:5, 9–12 = Ruth 4:18–22

Song of Songs
MT: Expansionistic
LXX: Literal translation, non-idiomatic Greek (B); *kaige* revision in B
Scrolls: 6QCant (1:1–7)

Ecclesiastes
MT: Expansionistic
LXX: Literal and mechanical translation in B (probably Aquila)
Scrolls: 4QQoh[a] (5:13–17; 6:3–8; 7:7–9)

Lamentations
MT: Expansionistic
LXX: Literal translation, non-idiomatic Greek (B); *kaige* revision in B
Scrolls: 3QLam (1:10–12; 3:53–62); 5QLam[a] (4:5–8, 11–16, 19–20; 4:20—5:13, 16–17); 5QLam (4:17–20)

Esther
MT: Expansionistic
LXX: Generally free translation (B); numerous larger and smaller additions in B not found in MT; also, many words in MT lacking in B; Lucianic witnesses include b and e$_2$ (Cambridge LXX = 19+108 and 93 Göttingen LXX); hexaplaric revision in all manuscripts
Papyri: Chester Beatty P. 967 and 968 (chaps. 2—8)

Daniel
MT: Expansionistic
LXX: *Kaige* (?) revision in B and all manuscripts except the corrupt Codex Chrisianus (C = 87/88), which is OG (with some hexaplaric readings); B: literal translation, non-idiomatic Greek; C: free but nonparaphrastic translation, idiomatic Greek; Syro-Hexapla important for the reconstruction of the OG
Papyri: Chester Beatty P. 967 (chaps. 3—8), a pre-hexaplaric witness to the OG
Scrolls: 1QDan[a] (1:10–17; 2:2–6); 1QDan[b] (3:22–31); 6QDan (8:16–17[?], 20–21[?]; 10:8–16; 11:33–36, 38)

Ezra
MT: Expansionistic
LXX: Literal translation, non-idiomatic Greek (B); *kaige* revision in B

Nehemiah
MT: Expansionistic
LXX: Literal translation, non-idiomatic Greek (B); *kaige* revision in B

1 and 2 Chronicles
MT: Expansionistic
LXX: Literal translation, non-idiomatic Greek (B); *kaige* revision in B, generally a troubled text; Lucianic witnesses, including the minuscules be$_2$y (Cambridge LXX), important for reconstructing the OG, especially in view of the condition of B
OL: Lucianic, important for the reconstruction of OG, especially in view of the character and condition of LXX^B, but very little survives
Parallels: Extensive parallels or partial parallels in Genesis, Samuel, and Kings; lesser parallels in Exodus, Numbers, Joshua, Psalms, and Ruth